9/13/09

Dear Terry,

To a wonderful weekend - you gave us a terrific mini-holiday & this is a memory for your perfect mini-holiday at Sea Ranch -

Love Dolores

Terry,
I enjoyed getting to know you better And that you had a true "short" vacation with Deloras and I. Sea Ranch and The ART TOUR WAS A NICE Mini plateau as you TRANSITION TO THE NEXT Phase of your life. I Hope You AND Your family come back

Regards Budd

The DeYoung House

# THE QUEST FOR COMMUNITY

by Richard Sexton with contributing essays by Ray Oldenburg and William Turnbull, Jr.

CHRONICLE BOOKS
SAN FRANCISCO

The Sea Ranch, California

# PARALLEL UTOPIAS

Seaside, Florida

# D E D I C A T I O N

Dedicated to my daughters, Adrianne and Claire.

The future belongs to them.

I hope that it will be richly endowed with memorable places

and that they will have as many opportunities

to explore them as I have.

Library of Congress Cataloging-in-Publication Data:

Sexton, Richard.
    Parallel Utopias : sea ranch and seaside : the
quest for community/ by Richard Sexton ; essays by
William Turnbull and Ray Oldenburg.
          p.      cm.

Includes bibliographical references (p.) and index.

    ISBN 0-8118-0547-6
    1. New towns—United States—Planning.
    2. Planned communities—United States.
    3. Suburbs—United States—Planning.
    4. Automobiles—Social aspects—United States.
    5. Sea Ranch Condominium.
    6. Seaside Community Development Corporation
    (Seaside, Fla.)
    I. Title.
    HT169.57.U6S49  1996
    307.76'8'0975941—dc20
          94-41172
          CIP

Printed in Hong Kong.

Book and cover design by Mya Kramer Design

Cover inset photographs:
(top) Esherick's Hedgerow Houses, The Sea Ranch,
California; (bottom) Ruskin Place town houses,
Seaside, Florida

Distributed in Canada by Raincoast Books,
8680 Cambie St., Vancouver, B.C. V6P 6M9

10 9 8 7 6 5 4 3 2

Chronicle Books
85 Second Street
San Francisco, CA 94105

# C O N T E N T S

# Parallel

# UTOPIAS

RICHARD SEXTON

This book is about a quest and two places that each in its own way is an embodiment of it. The quest is for a meaningful and appropriate environment in which to live. Home and community, expressed in the archetypal terms of *dream home* and *ideal community,* are central to this concept. The quest for the dream home in the ideal community is firmly embedded in the American Dream. This ubiquitous phrase is used to describe goals widely hailed as attainable in the United States with greater ease than elsewhere: succeeding in your career, giving your children better opportunities than you had, and, the most common invocation, owning your home. The ultimate aim of this dream is to own not just any home, anywhere, but the dream home. The attributes of this home are as unique and diverse as America itself. But the quest does not end with a house on a parcel of land. It should also encompass community.

We all want a special house, a private realm that we can own, and ideally we should want to be connected to a community that is equally special—a public realm in which we feel we own an undivided interest. The dream is simple, but its permutations are complex. Is the vision of our dreams an urban row house in the city, a cottage in the country, a bungalow in a small town, or a grand suburban villa? The quest for the dream home in the ideal community is a complex, challenging, fantasy-laden search.

The term *dream home* has almost become a cliché. The concept of an ideal community, however, is largely ignored. We become absorbed with whether we should have a traditional or modern house, how many baths it should contain, or where the entertainment center should go. Meanwhile little thought is given to community. Real estate agents tell us there are three things to look for in buying a house: location, location, and location. Houses can always be altered and additions built, but the attributes of the community around the house are largely beyond individual control. We, therefore, need to think about the broader context of community before we think about any particular house within it.

Like all ideals, the ideal community is an archetype which guides us, a tangible concept which shapes the design process and helps to establish meaningful criteria for improving communities. To the planner, the ideal community is about town planning; to the politician, it is about a code of law; to the theologian, it is a moral code that gives the community expression. To the citizenry, the ideal community can be all these things and more.

In a way, each time a town planner spreads out drafting paper and begins to design a new subdivision for a real estate developer, an ideal community is being attempted, unless, of course, disingenuous intent has undermined the process. Regardless of constraints of time, money, or ability, the planner wants to make his or her community a superior one, not an ordinary one. Failure is not the goal. The historical tradition of the ideal community is that it *is* planned, the result of someone's vision and not the product of the natural evolution of incremental settlement patterns. Additionally, the history of the ideal community is frequently tied to escape from religious, ethnic, and political persecution. John Winthrop used appropriate biblical references when he told his fellow Pilgrims, "We must consider that we will be A City Upon a Hill, the eyes of all people upon us." The Pilgrims sought utopia in a wild and largely uncharted land. America ultimately became a nation of immigrants who came here seeking a new life in a new place, in the pursuit of what has come to be expressed as the American Dream.

From a practical standpoint, all new communities in America are planned. The natural evolution of the urban environment is a thing of the past, and has been for some time. Just as every home is designed, so is the community, of which the home is a building block. That most new communities don't seem to be planned is a function of the fact that there is little or no coordination among the private developers who are independently creating the residential, retail, and commercial components that make up the total package. Further, what passes for planning is typically nothing more than accommodating the automobile.

Since World War II, new American residential communities have been delivered in the form of the automobile suburb. For the last half century, the automobile suburb has been the community of the future—the built example of the ideal community schemes of the

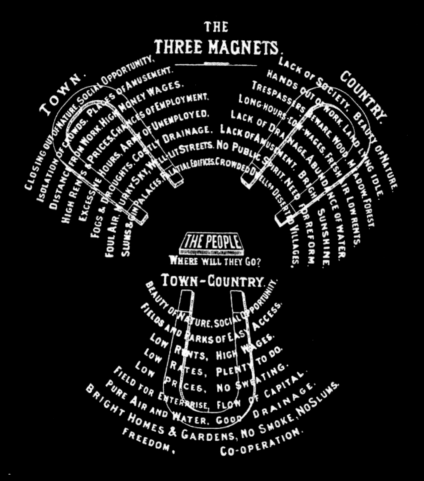

The Three Magnets
*by Sir Ebenezer Howard from*
*The Garden Cities of To-morrow*

postwar era. As the name implies, it is designed for automobile mobility and commuting. By the 1930s, middle-class ownership of automobiles had become increasingly common. They gave average Americans mobility and freedom at a level they had never before enjoyed. In the boom years after the war, with the Great Depression well over, middle-class auto ownership became pervasive.

The automobile had already become a central element in utopian visions of an ideal community in the decades before World War II. In the 1920s Le Corbusier proposed a model for future cities, which he called *Ville Radieuse* (Radiant City). In his plan, a grid of skyscrapers was laid out over a parklike landscape and connected by elevated motorways that allowed automobiles to drive directly into parking lots in the buildings. The density of the city was maintained, though the footprints of the tall buildings covered only about fifteen percent of the land. By 1935 in the United States, Frank Lloyd Wright answered Le Corbusier's *Ville Radieuse* with his own version of an ideal community centered on the automobile, which he called Broadacre City. This scheme was a fairly accurate prediction of what American automobile suburbia actually became. Wright proclaimed, "Let the auto take the city to the country." In Wright's model, low-slung architecture of complex form—modernistic evocations of the ranch house— were set back from the street, and landscaping was allowed to define and unify the streetscape. Major arterials of up to twelve lanes accommodated the automobile traffic.

*Edge City near New Orleans, Louisiana*

In the middle of the Depression, Wright's vision of a suburban ideal, where every adult owned a car, must have seemed far-fetched, but by the 1960s, the middle-class two-car family had become common. This was a critical development in automobile culture. Once both husband and wife had attained automobile mobility, the planning of the community could really change. The one-car family required that some planning attention be paid to the proximity of services, schools, and public transit. In the era of the two-car family, complete automobile mobility for all adults meant that the proximity of services could be measured in miles rather than blocks.

This mobility had a great impact on how developers could design new residential developments. A planned subdivision did not have to incorporate services or mass transit into its plan. Since residents could drive to obtain whatever they need, essential services could be located outside the community. This formula fostered homogeneity rather than diversity. There was little architectural diversity since the community contained only homes, and typically only single-family homes. It lacked socioeconomic diversity because only individuals who could afford to own a car for each adult in the household found it practical to live there. The poor, the elderly, the handicapped, young people beginning their careers, and anyone else who couldn't or didn't drive needed to live somewhere else.

Suburbia, including the manifestations that predate the automobile suburb, was originally conceived as being dependent on the city. The city had high-paying jobs and culture which could be reached by a "short" commute. The philosophical goal was to access all the good things that the city offered, while escaping the bad. It was not the intent of suburbia to be self-sufficient, though over time this has come to be the case. First came retail establishments in the form of strip centers and then came enclosed shopping malls. Both were distinctive for the acres of asphalt that encircled their low-rise architecture like an overscaled moat. Within the last couple of decades, commercial buildings have joined retail centers as a new presence in the suburban landscape. Suburban office parks, even commercial high-rise towers, are being built. Usually these suburban commercial hubs are located at key freeway or turnpike intersections.

Joel Garreau in his 1991 *Edge City: Life on the New Frontier,* coined the term *edge cities* to define these new retail and commercial agglomerations. *Suburb* no longer fully describes the built environment on the fringe of American cities. Some notable examples of this phenomenon are Silicon Valley near San Francisco; Tyson's Corner, Virginia, near Washington, D.C.; and the intersection of I-75 and Perimeter Road (I-285) near Atlanta. These developments are relatively new and their future evolution is the subject of debate. It is safe to say, however, that edge cities are nothing like the traditional commercial cores of American cities and that they are fundamentally changing the character of suburbs. Some urban historians define the advent of edge cities as signifying the demise of suburbia since the basic suburban precept of dependency on the traditional city is violated.

Although edge cities are a new phenomenon, suburbs certainly are not. Robert Fishman, in *Bourgeois Utopias: The Rise and Fall of Suburbia,* places the origin of the suburb in late eighteenth century London, where merchants, like their peers in other trades, conducted business from their homes: typically, multistoried urban row houses in the center of the city. The ground floor was the office or storefront from which business was transacted. Above the ground floor were the living quarters for the family. The wife usually was intimately involved with the business, since it was transacted under the same roof, if not in her presence. Home life and livelihood were intimately and, it would seem, inseparably intertwined.

So hectic was life in bustling London that prosperous merchants leased or purchased villas in the countryside to which they escaped on weekends. Their villas emulated, in more modest scale and appointment, the country villas of the English aristocracy, whose grand estates dotted the countryside around London. The lifestyle of the English aristocracy was based upon a livelihood derived from the land on which their villas stood. These landholdings provided the aristocracy with substantial income, allowing a life of leisure. Their merchant neighbors were in a different situation. They had attained a level of affluence rivaling that of the aristocracy, but had to work hard daily to sustain it. This new class of individuals who possessed the wealth of the aristocracy, but who invested as much time and energy in the workplace as tradesmen, came to be defined as the bourgeoisie, the merchant class, frequently synonymous with the upper middle class in the United States.

Weekend sojourns in the country gave the bourgeoisie a taste of the aristocratic English country life. As roads improved and their businesses continued to prosper, the bourgeoisie embarked on a new lifestyle. The London merchant could live in his country villa and commute by private coach to conduct business downtown. The urban row house that formerly served as home and workplace, came to serve only the latter purpose. The merchant's family could enjoy, on a full-time basis, a lifestyle modeled very closely on that of the aristocracy. The merchant's only sacrifice was that it took about thirty minutes to commute to work in the morning and thirty minutes to return home in the afternoon—a seemingly small sacrifice for a life of privilege in the country. To be near other merchants with similar country estates was certainly acceptable, even desirable, for the prestige inferred. Communities made up of bourgeois villas began to take shape.

The merchant's dream home was the opulent country villa modeled on Palladio's *Villa Rotonda* surrounded by grand formal gardens— a setting that Robert Fishman likens to "a house set in a park." Lawn maintenance was viewed as one's most important civic duty, for these individual lawns merged visually to create the collective park view that the villas enjoyed. Life in the countryside was by no means intended to be a life in the wilderness.

An essential function of these early suburbs was the effective segregation of the bourgeoisie from the "lowlife" of the city, just as the aristocracy used the country life to segregate themselves from commoners. By comparison, the preindustrial city from which the bourgeoisie were escaping afforded almost no class segregation—"whores and royalty" commingled, and wealthy merchants shared their back alleys with paupers. The segregation of social classes and the absence of the socioeconomic diversity found in urban settings remained integral to the evolving suburb. By moving to the suburbs, the bourgeoisie sought to escape the city, though they remained dependent on it—the husband tended his business, the wife shopped, and the children were educated there. The goal of their newfound community was to provide a life of privilege in a setting that was calmer, more pastoral, and ostensibly superior for childrearing, than the city.

Early in its evolution, the suburban ideal made its way to the United States. As American cities grew and became increasingly industrialized in the nineteenth century, the presence of ever-larger factories produced the need for a greater separation between work and home. One of the significant planning achievements of the late nineteenth century was the realization that a separation between residential and commercial environments lessened the spread of disease and improved the quality of life for the residential sector. The option of suburban living, and escape from the urban condition where residences were increasingly subordinated to an unsavory and overscaled workplace, was pursued by many who could afford it.

These nineteenth century suburbs were called streetcar suburbs, so named because they were developed along streetcar lines that residents used to commute to the commercial core of the city where they worked. Streetcar suburbs were almost always modeled after small towns. Their density was lower than that of the city, but the houses tended to have small street setbacks, or sometimes no setbacks, and were relatively close together. Land use was efficient since no one wanted to walk too far to reach the streetcar. Retail services were within the community, usually right on the streetcar line. These retail districts were essentially the downtown of the community.

Streetcar suburbs were integral to the development of new American communities for about a century until the Great Depression brought new housing construction to a virtual standstill. After World War II, the automobile firmly established itself on the American scene, and the approach to designing communities changed dramatically to accommodate it. For the past half century the American Dream increasingly has focused on seeking a better life in suburbia. The automobile is the technological innovation that facilitated this lifestyle option and is the integral component around which contemporary suburbia is designed. The question becomes, Is automobile suburbia the most refined expression of the ideal community that American society is capable of attaining? Automobile suburbia has its merits. The detached single-family house presents a clearly delineated image of home. The single-family house is the overwhelming preference when measured against other common types of housing. The suburban home provides a connection to the earth and a generous portion of private open space. The package, at its most basic level, is affordable for the lower middle class. In spite of all this, automobile suburbia tends to be too watered-down: it lacks the diversity and urbanity of the city, while failing to provide enough of the beauty and tranquillity of the natural environment. An automobile-dependent community, segregated from retail and commercial uses and generally lacking in architectural and socioeconomic diversity, is no utopia.

At the fundamental level, community is about sharing—sharing space, amenities, and a public realm—as well as sharing the responsibility and duty necessary to ensure their well-being. The formative stages of community development in the United States were galvanized by the common pursuit of survival in a new and potentially hostile environment. Community was further bolstered by the desire for political, cultural, and religious freedoms. Those early American towns admired for their urban fabric firmly anchored in the concept of community—intimate scale, contextual architecture, and an urbanity as efficient as it was compassionate—were not the products of a society more enlightened than that of postwar America. Rather, their residents gained, through mutual sacrifice and cooperation, desperately needed security and civic amenities. They enhanced their lives as they built good communities. Participation was more mandatory than voluntary, options were basic, and both homes and communities reflected this situation. Community was a vital resource for the individual. It mattered.

Over many ensuing decades, the battle for survival and freedom was largely won, and American citizens were rewarded with relative financial prosperity and generous political freedoms. The United States likely boasts a more empowered private citizen than can be found in any other culture, past or present. Amid this great triumph of empowerment for the individual, communities tended to devolve. Americans are no longer so dependent on their fellow citizens and on cooperative effort for survival, and the collective good has been sacrificed at the altar of self-fulfillment. Contemporary American society is fixated to a fault on the generous freedom granted the individual, while the collective concept of community languishes in apathy. In postwar America, it just has not mattered as it once did.

Automobile suburbia is a manifestation of the devolution of community from a shared realm with shared purpose to an amalgamation of closely bunched, independent mini-estates. As author and urban sociologist Ray Oldenburg observes in *The Great Good Place,* residents of suburbia try to own individually what a community once provided for all. They don't share, but hoard, as each homesite seeks to be a self-sufficient entity. Better communities might surface, but only if the empowered individual is aware and desirous of them, even in need of them. As architect and writer Alex Krieger has observed, "We admire one kind of place, but we consistently build something very different, the more familiar sprawl of suburbia." Added impetus for building communities like those we admire will come from the fact that we are running out of suitable land and the money to create and sustain the gargantuan infrastructure required by the continued building of automobile suburbia.

The attitude of sharing vital to the residents of a community must extend to its architecture. Shared attitudes toward architectural attributes like scale, setbacks, building materials, and roofs must exist for the built environment to have coherence. Having shared attitudes about architectural elements within the built environment is different from advocating sameness—the mass production of identical houses. Sameness of architecture at the scale of an entire community fosters disorientation and boredom. In automobile suburbia, residential neighborhoods are plagued by architectural sameness. As edge cities came on the scene, their commercial and retail buildings were disparate in scale and bore little relationship to each other or the residential communities around them.

*St. Charles Avenue streetcar*
*New Orleans, Louisiana*

Memorable communities are defined by the vitality of their public forum as much as by the beauty of their geographic setting or the elegance of their architecture. The ideal community should afford the opportunity for all types of social interaction, as well as the opportunity to have privacy and be free from association when it is not desired. Ray Oldenburg articulates an important attribute of community: "We are an associating species whose nature is to share space just as we share experiences; few hermits are produced in any human culture. A habitat that discourages association, one in which people withdraw to privacy as turtles into their shells, denies community and leaves people lonely in the midst of many."

Places where people can congregate informally are not just a function of the urban experience in larger towns and cities. Small towns and settlements have them as well. There's the bench in front of the general store where locals gather and share sodas and small talk. The filling station and the seed-and-feed store in rural communities can be similar meeting places. Other gathering places have no architectural presence—the sandlot where kids gather to play ball, the open field where townspeople like to walk their dogs and exchange pleasantries. One of the most notable public places lacking any architectural dimension is found in coastal communities: the beach. The special ambience that so many beach communities have is attributable to the presence of the beach and its vigorous public realm that is a setting for elaborate rituals of social interaction.

A major debate continues among planners as to whether human behavior and interaction can be affected positively by the creation of a built environment that attempts to promote or encourage social interaction. This concept has come to be identified as architectural determinism or socially deterministic planning. If parks, playgrounds, community centers, and similar facilities are placed within residential neighborhoods, will their presence make residents more friendly toward one another and likely to interact more often? This is the crux of the socially deterministic planning debate. There is considerable evidence that socially deterministic planning is effective, but even one of its most notable proponents, Peter Calthorpe, in his 1993 book, *The Next American Metropolis*, points out that this subject has been endlessly debated "to no conclusive result." The difficulty is in determining whether cultural predilections were responsible for enhanced social interaction in certain places, or whether the presence of an architectural forum led to a heightened level of social interaction. It is a classic debate over which factor came first, the conducive architectural forum or the cultural desire for it.

A key characteristic of social interaction, first elucidated by Jane Jacobs in her 1961 book, *The Death and Life of Great American Cities*, helps clarify the extent to which the built environment may influence social interaction. People interact with one another on two levels, a casual, or informal, level and an intimate level. Casual interaction is the type you may have with the proprietor of the corner store, a neighbor, or a mail carrier. You may have known each other for years, yet never have considered going out to dinner together. Neither party feels snubbed because your interaction was always intended to be casual. Intimate interaction is different. It is spawned typically by strong common interests and may be maintained across great physical distances. Dinner invitations and social evenings together are expected.

The extent to which the architectural environment influences social interaction relates to the casual type, and automobile suburbia is specifically deprived of it. Neighbors don't readily get to know each other, and they rarely bump into each other during the course of their daily lives. Even though there are people inside the homes, the neighborhoods always seem devoid of activity. Intimate interaction is relatively unaffected, however, and nothing that the planner may do is going to change this very much. Two people who have little in common are not going to become good friends just because they live in adjacent row houses facing a plaza, rather than in two detached ranch houses facing a curving street that they experience only from behind the wheel of a car. However, the former setting may greatly enhance their casual social interaction as neighbors sharing space and experiences within it.

Regardless of the potential influence of socially deterministic planning, it is an observable phenomenon that the more comfortable, self-sufficient, and grand the private home becomes, the less time its residents are likely to spend in the public forum. As trends have been established in the United States, most notably private affluence and public poverty, people tend to overindulge in their homes to offset the deficiency of the broader context of the community in which they live.

*Stoop sitters, French Quarter*
*New Orleans, Louisiana*

In the ideal community, architecture should be human-scaled, not high-rise. As Christopher Alexander observes in *A Pattern Language*, buildings taller than about four stories begin to lose their humanity and place their occupants in an artificial environment. Most people don't like to be in extremely tall buildings for extended periods because they feel divorced from the earth, to which they want to be connected. Lewis Mumford likewise strongly criticized the skyscraper in *The Culture of Cities* as subordinating human concerns to pecuniary interests. The modern technical innovation of the skyscraper allowed thousands of square feet of commercial or residential space to be developed on very small urban parcels. Minimal land purchases could be parlayed into grand developments in the commercial core of a city. This high-rise landscape came to define the modern metropolis. The commercial core of the city, a very small area geographically, became the workplace for tens and hundreds of thousands of workers. Is it only coincidence that once workers were packed into an ever-smaller high-rise

*Decatur Street, French Quarter*
*New Orleans, Louisiana*

workplace, suburban living became the preferred choice as a place of residence? The overdeveloped commercial core begot the underdeveloped suburb. When placed in an extremely dense work setting, most workers chose to put more space around themselves in the one setting over which they had great control: their residence. The average worker likely will continue to choose to live at, or below, the density of automobile suburbia, unless cities become more human-scaled through judicious use of extremely tall buildings and decentralization of the commercial core. Work and residence need to be better integrated so that both can coexist, as they once did, within the same self-sufficient neighborhood.

The ideal community should be inclusive, not exclusive. There should be a place within it for everyone who wants to belong. Ideal communities and the dream homes within them should be as diverse as their residents. Yet the whole should be harmonious and not discordant. Diversity is one of the most important characteristics of communities. As communities become larger, their diversity tends to increase. The reward of greater diversity offsets some of the sacrifices, such as the loss of private open space and the need in a high-density community to live in a small home or apartment. Diversity of all kinds is a key attraction of cities: the varied style and scale of the architecture; the rich mix of ethnicity, background, and social type of the population; the multitudinous choices in every aspect from shopping and dining to career potential. Perhaps no observer of the urban scene better articulated the importance of diversity than Jane Jacobs did in *The Death and Life of Great American Cities*.

As Jacobs observed, diversity is aided, or thwarted, by an eternal ebb and flow of common occurrences in the urban environment. Within retail districts, an important aid to diversity is the presence of buildings of varying age and condition. A trendy new restaurant may be able to support the high rent that a new or fully restored and updated building may command, but a local cleaner or used-book store may not. Also promoting the diversity of a neighborhood are amenities that serve different functions for different people over the course of the day. A park, for instance, can be a place for supervised play for toddlers in the morning, an afterschool playground for older children in the afternoon, and a place for an intimate stroll for young couples in the evening. The park is used throughout the day and evening and accommodates a wide mix of individuals. It also encourages retail diversity because the people whom it attracts support a broader mix of businesses than might exist if this amenity were not present.

Jacobs makes a profound observation about the diversity of neighborhoods: failure can be brought on by prosperity. Neighborhoods that become too prosperous actually lose diversity. Overly regentrified residential and shopping districts are not as interesting as less prosperous ones that are capable of supporting both a broader socioeconomic mix of residents and a wider variety of retail establishments. Overly ambitious regentrification or development tends to be exclusive, which at first may seem positive. Ultimately, however, inclusiveness and the rich variety of human experience it nurtures make for more interesting communities. As architect and planner Leon Krier points out, anything not expressly prohibited should not only be allowed, but be encouraged. One of the major problems of automobile suburbia is that it is too exclusive and is generally lacking in true socioeconomic diversity. Exclusivity has been, from the very beginning, at the core of the suburban ideal. Vincent Scully sums up the situation found in automobile suburbia in *American Architecture and Urbanism:*

*American purism used European purism to serve its own ends, which were of a perfect, cityless, endlessly suburban world, to which anyone could belong who possessed the following qualifications: (a) enough money to build his own house and operate a car or two, and (b) the right color (once the right religion, too, but that requirement largely passed by) to be allowed to build in the suburbs at all. If one was poor (of whom there were comparatively few in America) or black (there were about the same number), there was no room in the dreamworld for him. Since a majority has been able to meet middle-class standards in the United States, it has usually been simply tough luck for those who couldn't; they have never controlled enough power, upon which architecture is ultimately based, to build a reasonable environment for themselves. They resentfully make use of the leftovers or are put up in barracks, their wishes unconsulted; and they are otherwise never included in the ideal environmental schemes—to make room for which, in fact, they are normally removed.*

The suburban tradition has further bolstered economic means as the primary determinant of social standing within the community. In the preindustrial city, how much you earned and how you earned it were equally obvious and were factors in the social status your peers conferred upon you. In the work-segregated suburb, how you attain your wealth is far less significant than how much of it you have. The only government-sponsored, socially condoned form of discrimination in the United States—economic discrimination—is supported by the suburban lifestyle. This kind of discrimination tends to promote a culture where income potential is a key factor in career decisions and to fuel materialism as the predominant measure of attainment. The infatuation with making a lot of money is explained to a great extent by the cost of a suburban lifestyle. Town planner Andres Duany cites a statistic that a suburban household requires two cars, each costing an average of five thousand dollars per year to operate. The suburban householder spends, on average, six weeks of leisure time commuting to and from work, which should be measured against the two weeks, on average, of paid vacation each year. An alternative lifestyle that requires only one car for a middle-class family and eliminates commuting translates to a raise of five thousand dollars and the addition of six weeks of quality time annually. With this potential reward, alternatives are worth exploring in an ideal community where home and work are integrated and community standing is based not just on financial attainment.

The ideal community should be convenient. Basic needs should be close by and easy to reach, preferably by walking. Again, it was Jacobs who understood this dynamic and articulated it well. She emphasized the need for "a sufficiently dense concentration of people . . . concentration produces convenience." A neighborhood with low density can support few local businesses. To be able to walk to a pharmacy, corner grocery, dry cleaner, or hardware store is viable only in a neighborhood with enough residents clustered closely enough together to support the businesses. Without these businesses, residents have to commute to another neighborhood to find vital goods and services. High density should not be regarded, as it frequently is, as a universal negative. If a high-density neighborhood is correctly planned, everything the residents give up in the way of personal space should be complemented by the addition of conveniences they

*Bourbon Street, French Quarter
New Orleans, Louisiana*

would not have otherwise had. This formula ensures that neighborhoods of greater and lesser density enjoy relatively equal desirability. One problem in automobile suburbs is the lack of adequate density to support a wide array of neighborhood retailing and a viable system of public transit within the community. Because of this, residents must drive to a mall supported by many neighborhoods. The convenience of obtaining basic needs by walking, rather than by driving, is an issue vital to the quality and convenience of an urban life.

The advent of the automobile is typically depicted by urban observers as troublesome, particularly because it promoted sprawl in American communities. The point may be well taken, but it fails to acknowledge that the automobile, in and of itself, is worthwhile. It gave freedom and mobility to the middle class and made lives easier in many ways. It drew people to the open road to explore America and connected families in the countryside to the towns that served them. The problem is not automobiles, but automobile abuse. A particularly problematic manifestation of automobile abuse is the remaking of the built environment with the single design goal of accommodating the automobile while giving only cursory design attention to other human concerns. To plan for the automobile is smart. To plan *only* for the automobile is not, because it promotes the abuse of an otherwise worthwhile achievement. The pedestrian is not very important in a world scaled and oriented exclusively to the automobile. The bulk of the planning effort in designing the ideal community should be focused on creating a place that is compelling for the walker. No one walks in automobile suburbia, not just because it's impractical, but also because it's unpleasant. Rather than depress themselves by attempting an errand by walking, people just get in the car and turn up the stereo.

The ideal community should incorporate nature, in some form, within its bounds. Parks, town squares, street trees, and landscaped medians of divided roadways are common elements in urban settings. When complemented by the private garden, these elements soften the built environment and bring nature into the city. Lewis Mumford stated in *The Culture of Cities* that "parks and gardens are not luxuries for the fortunate minority: they are essential if the city is to become a permanent habitat for man. . . . What the baroque planner gave to the palace and the upper class residential quarter alone, we now conceive as essential for every part of the city."

There is broad acceptance among architects and planners that cities and towns, down to the smallest settlements, need to incorporate something of the natural environment within their bounds, but there is debate over how nature should be manifested in the built environment. As architect William Turnbull observed in an interview, the oft-proposed greenbelts surrounding towns and settlements cannot consist of fallow, unmanaged land. The problem, he states, is not with the deer grazing in the meadow. It is with the mountain lion that stalks and kills the deer as it grazes in our meadow. This scene we may find regrettable, but that young children could also be prey we find intolerable. We demand some control over large predators because we ultimately don't like what they do. Fires occur naturally in the forest. They are good for the forest, but they destroy habitat—including homes and public buildings adjacent to unmanaged land. If we desire to live in the wilderness, or to allow wilderness to adjoin or permeate the built environment, it has to be managed, and we cannot pretend that we are not a part of it. Nature has to be given meaningful context and expression, if the quality of life in communities is going to be enhanced by its presence. Ecological issues are a significant component of the community planning debate.

The indigenous landscape should be taken into account when nature is incorporated into communities. One of the great environmental disasters in automobile suburbia stems from the notion that landscaping should be more or less the same whether it is in suburban Illinois or southern California. The endless cadence of suburban lawns and backyard swimming pools in the greater Los Angeles area has made the region more humid as residents artificially support a landscape that has no place in a desert. That they consume water from northern California and Arizona to help support their artificial landscape only makes things worse. Indigenous landscaping does not require artificial support under ordinary circumstances and always seems more natural because it is. One of the great achievements of automobile suburbia is the provision for a generous amount of private open space, but the entire effort is wasted when a natural landscape is supplanted by one that must be sustained artificially at great cost.

The fundamental building block of community is the house—the private residence. In the ideal community, the design of the houses should involve those who will live in them. Individuals who will call the house *home*—whether it is new construction or the modification of an existing dwelling—should be permitted to participate in the process. The independently commissioned custom home involves its owners in the design process and makes them patrons of architecture. They gain insight into the creation of home and community. A similar owner involvement with existing houses ensures that new owners can live in old houses as effectively and efficiently as those who commissioned them.

Building the custom home and significantly modifying the older home have been hampered by modern municipalities with befuddling, byzantine bureaucracies that move at reptilian pace and adhere to vague standards decided upon through some arcane process, the decisions of which are subject to seemingly endless appeals. As a result, in many large metropolitan areas independent commissioning of the custom home is dying out. Individual initiative has been replaced by developers who build generic tract homes targeted at the theoretical generic family. This has become the only choice for most home buyers. Commissioning a custom home can be simplified if a community sets broad parameters, is forthright about what is and isn't allowed, and then grants dictatorial control to the bureaucratic body empowered to enforce the rules. As undemocratic as this alternative may sound, it is better than the process that largely excludes owner involvement and results in the tract home as the only choice. The continued viability of the custom home is also important to the storefront architectural practice, which has been in sad decline. Architects are increasingly working for real estate developers, and only the extremely wealthy are able to commission their own homes.

Perhaps the greatest achievement of the suburban experience is that it has allowed so many people to own their homes. For many of these people, home ownership is a lifelong goal and the ultimate symbol of attainment. Christopher Alexander states in *A Pattern Language*, "People cannot be genuinely comfortable and healthy in a house which is not theirs." For something as important as this is, the user must be included. One of the problems with automobile suburbia is the cookie-cutter approach to design, resulting in

*Upper Grant Avenue, North Beach*
*San Francisco, California*

neighborhoods filled with houses whose occupants were allowed little participation. To no one's surprise, these occupants often have a dispassionate attitude toward their homes and neighborhoods. People who have been given little input in the design of their homes typically understand little about their communities.

The choice of building materials is very important to the realization of the dream home. How a material ages is significant to this choice. Dents in old aluminum siding are altogether different from the silvery patina of a weathered redwood board. Choosing materials solely because they last a "lifetime," that is, twenty-five years with considerable luck, overlooks the aesthetic issues that ensure long-term satisfaction with a house. An appreciation for fine craftsmanship is equally important. We have largely come to expect houses to be thrown together with an increasing propensity to combine shoddy workmanship with even shoddier materials, and we tend to think that only an old house can satisfy our desire for quality workmanship and materials. This doesn't have to be the case. To be affordable, new houses may have to be simple and smaller, and the suburban program of one household per lot may have to be breached, but houses shouldn't have to be built shoddily from inappropriate materials. Low-maintenance may be the deciding factor in deciding between two appropriate materials, but should not be the primary reason for choosing a material. The honesty of a material is also important. Camouflaged materials like cultured marble, laminated paneling, wood-grain laminates, and linoleum patterned to look like ceramic tile are seldom as satisfying over the long term as the same materials without all the disguises. When plastics, plywood, laminate, and linoleum are designed to take advantage of their inherent qualities, they are almost always better than when they are made to resemble another material.

*Tree Fern Forest, Golden Gate Park*
*San Francisco, California*

The dream home should be responsive to the climate in which it is located. In the Deep South, for instance, domestic buildings historically were characterized by generous porches, operable, louvered shutters, and tall ceilings. The porch shaded the interior rooms and allowed windows to remain open in the hot summer even with the constant threat of thunderstorms. Shutters permitted air circulation, but kept light out, reducing passive solar heating. Closed shutters provided security in urban homes while allowing windows to be left open at night or when the house was briefly unattended. Tall ceilings provided a volumetric space for hot air to escape to a level above the bounds of human activity. All these architectural features were intended to make the house more comfortable in a hot, humid climate. Over time, a different appreciation of these functional elements emerged. The porch became integral to southern culture and social interaction. Shutters became a desired aesthetic component of the house. Tall ceilings came

to infer grandeur. These and many other regional distinctions in traditional American architecture are not based solely on cultural and historical predilections, but on climate. The grand overscaled hearth of the Prairie house provided warmth and symbolized comfort through the midwestern winter; the saltbox plan of the New England house modified a medieval English prototype so that more interior room was available for indoor life during the cold winter; the sleeping porches on California bungalows took advantage of the cool, fresh breezes from the Pacific.

Technology has facilitated a common functional approach to architectural design regardless of climactic considerations. The development of mechanized central heating and cooling has made the house insular year-round. Those architectural elements developed to make a house comfortable in its climate are deemed unnecessary. In the Deep South, the tradition of tall ceilings, operable shutters, and grand porches has been replaced by ranch-house functionality: eight-foot ceilings, inoperable shutters, air-conditioning, and nominal entry porches barely larger than a doormat. The house is reduced to a stereotype suitable for any climate. An equally frightening aspect of this evolution is the decline and misappropriation of regionalism in domestic architecture. In automobile suburbia, the ranch house is used pervasively. In its original form, this rural house type was a beautiful regional expression of the American Southwest. Given only token regional embellishments and an ersatz natural landscape, it fills automobile suburbs across the country.

Climate responsiveness affects not only our homes. It also affects public and commercial buildings. The architectural grandeur of public spaces like the imposing rotunda of city hall, the large volumetric space of a railway station, the soaring atrium of an opulent hotel has been in decline, due not so much to the prohibitive cost of construction, but to the prohibitive cost of maintaining climate control. As Venturi, Scott Brown, and Izenour observed in *Learning From Las Vegas*, low, horizontal, single-story buildings

can be air-conditioned and heated much more cost-effectively than vertical, multistoried buildings with complex interior volumetric spaces. At every turn grandeur is sacrificed for creature comforts facilitated by complex mechanical systems.

As important as the attributes of a home's architecture are the objects we choose to put in it. Despite broad efforts to trivialize what is commonly referred to as "decor," the possessions that personalize the dream home could not be more important. These objects are the artifacts of our lives: they reflect our passions for collecting, our interests, our goals, our achievements. Christopher Alexander, in *A Pattern Language*, summarizes this with great eloquence when he states the following.

*The things around you should be the things that mean most to you, which have the power to play a part in the continuous process of self-transformation, which is your life . . . But this function has been eroded, gradually, in modern times because people have begun to look outward, to others, and over their shoulder, at the people who are coming to visit them, and have replaced their natural instinctive decorations with the things which they believe will please and impress their visitors. . . . But the irony is, that the visitors who come into a room don't want this nonsense any more than the people who live there. It is far more interesting to come into a room which is the living expression of a person. . . .*

A design professional can certainly assist the personal decisions that a homeowner may make. But interior designers, in their most worthwhile commissions at least, do not independently fabricate environments into which the individual is then randomly deposited. In their defense, interior designers plug homeowners into fabricated, formulaic environments far less pervasively than real estate developers plug them into cookie-cutter suburban developments.

## BEYOND AUTOMOBILE SUBURBIA

The utopian quest for the dream home in the ideal community becomes, in pragmatic terms, the attempt to achieve the best home possible—a home that is appropriate, functional, and aesthetically pleasing, in a community that provides convenience, stimulation, and fulfillment. At the scale of a contemporary national population, the search for the dream home in the ideal community can largely be defined as finding something better than automobile suburbia. Yet the pursuit of the American Dream has found the majority of people living in a single-family house in suburbia and feeling that this is the best they are likely to achieve.

Government has long been subsidizing home ownership in automobile suburbia as the most appropriate fulfillment of the American Dream, while ignoring both our cities and our natural environment. Most of the infrastructure in the public realm consists of roads and freeways, rather than parks and public buildings. Financing requirements from the Federal Housing Administration and the Veterans Administration and the development of the thirty-year mortgage fueled the relentless expansion of automobile suburbia. Society, particularly the middle class, has extolled suburban living as the archetypal solution to one's lifestyle needs. Suburbanites typically seem to have little yearning for a meaningful relationship with the city or the country as they flirt with both and then return to suburbia to live. In this scenario, the ideal community seems insignificant. Only the dream home really matters.

As a society, we fixate on the dream home and not on the ideal community for reasons that are driven largely by circumstance. We frequently feel that the choice of community is predicated on where we can earn a living, the availability and affordability of housing, and numerous other factors external to us. As James Howard Kunstler observes in *The Geography of Nowhere*, it is the educated classes who will readily relocate to advance their careers. Yet it is this very same class of individuals, so quick to dispose of their current community to further their own causes, that is so preoccupied with the dream home. Emerging factors may begin to change this, however.

The need to be at a specific workplace, for specific hours, working in concert with fellow employees, has long been integral to employment. This requirement was largely a function of the industrial age. In the emerging postindustrial age, as American businesses and the workforce have changed, Americans are increasingly employed in the service sector. The mass media is largely fixated on the negative implications of postindustrialism, but these changes have a positive side that should not be ignored. Although we are manufacturing fewer widgets, we aren't just flipping more burgers. We are increasingly consulting, advising, planning, and administering as well. Many service sector employers that require a trained, highly educated workforce have begun to express more enlightened attitudes toward working arrangements through such policies as flextime, provisions for working at home, and research sabbaticals. Employment requirements and lifestyle choices in the postindustrial age are becoming quite different from those of America's industrial era. We may not get more money for what we do, but we can get something better: a higher quality of life.

If information and work product rather than a huge workforce were moved around, many people could live and work in an environment chosen for its character and not its proximity to the workplace. Computer networks, modems, faxes, telephones, and couriers can move documents and information more cost-effectively than transit systems can move a large workforce. This is the transit system of high-tech, service sector employment. Writers, artists, software programmers, sales representatives, and many others, because of the nature of their work, can already choose where they live with greater freedom from career constraints than they ever could before. A wide range of urban-professionals may soon be able to make this choice. In the December 1993 *Progressive Architecture*, editor Thomas Fisher observes: "As both production and consumption become less and less dependent upon the physical proximity of coworkers or merchandise, people will become increasingly free to live anywhere along the information highway. And as that freedom becomes more prevalent, the quality of life in a place . . . may become the dominant criterion for choosing one's residence." To make this possibility a reality, we need to broaden our appreciation of community. Indeed, that we may soon live wherever we want is frightening unless we consider the concept of community. Otherwise, the information highway is sure to finish off the process that automobile abuse began. The information highway already is being marketed as a lifestyle fix for the inherent inconveniences of an atomized life in automobile suburbia—an undesirable fix that precludes the rebirth of traditional community.

Over the past century Americans have pervasively redistributed themselves. Christopher Alexander, in *A Pattern Language*, cites the statistic that "only 100 years ago 85 percent of the Americans lived on rural land; today 70 percent live in cities." The massive migration from rural to urban areas over the past several decades was driven by jobs. Individuals saw expanding job opportunities in the city as they witnessed shrinking opportunities in small towns and rural areas. Many who live in urban or suburban areas but might prefer to live elsewhere remain where they are because of their careers. On weekends and during vacations and in their retirement, they make their way back to the small town or the country where the environment stimulates and energizes them. This is where they've wanted to be all along. To the extent that the postindustrial age affords it, many people may be able to live in the countryside or in small towns *and* work there. The information highway will enable those in the countryside to have many of the choices of their urban peers. Shopping electronically via computer networks will probably be as popular for future countryside residents as mail-order catalogs were for rural residents in the early twentieth century when, thanks to the post office, rural free delivery succeeded in better connecting them to the rest of the world.

Because most people will not abandon the city and move to the countryside, ultimately we must address the familiar criticisms of urban life. The metropolitan areas of our largest cities encompass several counties and scores of municipalities. Commuting by automobile has become a burdensome chore. We are running out of places to park our cars at work, at home, and when running errands. More roads, more freeways, and more parking lots have led only to more cars and an entrenched dependency on the automobile. The quality of urban life is deteriorating with the infrastructure of our cities. Our cities and urban neighborhoods need new investment. I feel strongly that the pattern that began with the emergence of the automobile suburb after World War II is nearing an end. As the predominant pattern of middle-class urban living, it has reached the point of severely diminishing returns. Furthermore, it is apparent to politician and planner alike that automobile suburbia is not sustainable and is no longer a viable model for the future growth of our largest cities. In a free society, it makes sense to subsidize a full array of lifestyle choices. For the last half century, we've done the opposite. We've subsidized the choice of automobile suburbia, above all other options, and are faced with urban decay, stagnant rural communities, and a countryside littered with abandoned homesteads and environmental disasters.

As we approach a new millennium, we face the prospect of greater freedom in choosing where and how we live, facilitated by a changing workplace and new technologies that will support it, and the need to address the deficiencies of the urban environment. To keep the American Dream alive and prospering, we need new solutions. An appropriate beginning is to seek out promising prototypes, the subject matter of this work.

The two communities I have cast as prototypes in this work are different, yet similar places: The Sea Ranch, California, and

Seaside, Florida. These two communities provide the opportunity to illustrate a wide range of issues that articulate the contemporary search for the dream home in the ideal community. As with any work that uses case studies to explore broad issues, the particular becomes a vehicle for understanding the general. Sea Ranch and Seaside reflect drastically different priorities, approach their goals differently, and arrive at different solutions to common problems. Like Washington, D.C., and Brasilia, they have similar purposes and dissimilar programs for achieving them.

Both communities are located in striking geographical settings—the sorts of places that we imagine utopian places should be. Long before the built environment had made its presence felt, the locales of Sea Ranch and Seaside were special and memorable. Sea Ranch spans ten miles of rugged northern California coast, its rolling forested hills becoming precipitous cliffs as they meet the surf of the deep blue Pacific Ocean. Seaside is nestled into the low, scrubby flatlands of the Florida panhandle on the warm emerald waters of the Gulf of Mexico.

Sea Ranch and Seaside are communities that exist for the purpose of enriching the lives of their residents. Both communities consist primarily of second homes, and this offers a unique situation: Residents and visitors are there strictly by choice. They come to enrich their lives with memorable experiences in a memorable place, not for purposes of career or commerce, or by mere happenstance. Second-home communities are, by their very nature, more utopian minded than other communities. This is a significant asset in casting second-home communities as prototypes for the ideal community. Their liability is that they are divorced from the practical causal factors that create and sustain primary-home communities. However, recreation and relaxation are real needs, and leisure activities are the foundation of considerable commerce. Second-home communities support jobs, and in some cases these jobs are held by residents. The most significant factor in this debate is, I feel, the recognition that basic human needs and expectations in regard to home and community do not change simply because residents are on their leisure. If anything, these needs become more intensely focused. Historically, some of the most revered places and most successful attempts at building meaningful communities are resorts or retreats. That both Sea Ranch and Seaside have been developed recently—Sea Ranch in the mid-1960s and Seaside in the early 1980s—makes them particularly viable examples, for they were attained by and are culturally connected to contemporary American society.

Sea Ranch and Seaside have dual identities. On the one hand, each is a community created for those who live in it, and on the other, each is a model that may be applied, in whole or in part, to many different situations. This book explores both these identities. The best way to validate a community as a prototype is to show it as a meaningful type. The individual homes featured from each community were chosen for their effective combination of setting, architecture, furnishings, and decor. The age of the home within the community, the budget, the architectural style, and the lifestyle choices of its owners were also important factors in its inclusion. Some of the houses featured were built on limited budgets, are small in scale, and are furnished entirely with hand-me-downs. Other houses were built with grand budgets and have opulent appointments. Their common denominator is sensitivity and appropriateness, not budget or grandeur. Each home is featured for its fulfillment of the needs, desires, and aesthetic sensibilities of those whom it shelters.

Sea Ranch is a community inspired by the idealized country life. It is a development pattern that accommodates relatively large numbers of people (over twenty-three hundred homesites on about four thousand acres), but maintains the natural environment as the dominant impression. At Sea Ranch the natural environment determines appropriate design responses that are then applied to the built environment. This community realizes many of the goals promised, but not delivered, by the traditional automobile suburb. It does so by embracing traditional urban values *less* vigorously than contemporary suburbia.

Seaside, on the other hand, looks back to a time before World War II, when accommodating people, not the automobile, was the driving force in urban planning. There is at Seaside a deeply rooted sense of history and acknowledgment of the past. The architecture is human-scaled, and the architectural styles are rooted in familiar traditions. Like Sea Ranch, Seaside realizes key goals that contemporary suburbia has failed to deliver. It does so by embracing traditional urban values *more* vigorously than contemporary suburbia.

Sea Ranch and Seaside approach their utopian goals differently, and each manages to achieve something special. Their exact similarities are few. Differences in regional predilections, natural environment, and climate set the two communities apart. It is in this sense that they are *Parallel Utopias*. Yet their independently achieved results make for a compelling comparison. There is a certain polarity to Sea Ranch and Seaside, much like the distinction between country and town living, that makes them thought-provoking examples of community. Their distinctive approaches to planning issues, from the use of property-line fences, the layout of roads, and the siting of houses to the size of the lots and the style and type of the houses put upon them, stem from the fundamental differences between urban living and country living.

The polarity of Sea Ranch and Seaside is what first attracted my attention and begged comparison of the two places. I initially thought of them as opposites, but closer analysis has shown that they are anything but opposite. I've come to think of Sea Ranch and Seaside as being of the same species but of opposite gender. I've also come to think of them as representing a continuum. The manner in which each community rejected the status quo of automobile suburbia reflects the evolution of a generation of Americans. Both communities will endure, not only because of their accomplishments, but also because of the ways each reflects the distinctive time and place of its origin.

Sea Ranch and Seaside bring us closer to the ideal community. If this book, and the concepts embodied by the communities that are its subject, could be distilled to a single enduring message, it should be this: the dream home isn't worth much without an ideal community.

**America and its cities**

SUBurb no URBS ∘ BANlieu no LIEU ∘ FAUbourg no BOURG ∘ VORort no ORT

THE HANGMAN and its VICTIM
THE ANTI-CITY is out to KILL the CITY

CITY
and
LANDSCAPE
a good
MARIAGE

this City is no longer
a true City
this landscape no longer
a true LANDSCAPE
SUBURB ALWAYS
DEFEATS BOTH

a SUBURB
WITHOUT a
CITY
WILL FIND ITS VICTIM
at whatever EXPENSE
EFFORT or DISTANCE

**are at a crossroads.**

— *the beginning of the final report of the 82nd American Assembly, of Columbia University, on* Interwoven Destinies: Cities and the Nation. *April 15-18, 1993.*

# The Sea Ranch

LIVING LIGHTLY ON THE LAND

**THE SEA RANCH,** a planned coastal development in northern Sonoma County, spans about ten miles along the Pacific Ocean and recedes about one mile into the coastal hills. At the northern edge is the Gualala River, which meanders to the sea as it forms the border between Sonoma County and Mendocino County to the north. Sea Ranch is about one hundred miles north of the San Francisco Bay Area, but because of the terrain, it is reached by a car drive of about two and one-half hours. The last several miles along Highway 1, above the ocean, are precipitous and circuitous. Sacramento, the state capital, is only a little farther away from Sea Ranch than the Bay Area. The San Francisco Bay Area and the Sacramento area combined make up a population base of about six million people within a car drive of Sea Ranch. Nonetheless, the drive along Highway 1 and over the narrow road through the coastal range to the east of Sea Ranch renders it a remote location with limited access.

Just to the south of Sea Ranch is Stewart's Point, a small settlement with a general store, a post office, and a few houses and outbuildings clustered at the intersection of Highway 1 and Skaggs Springs Road. To the north of Sea Ranch is Gualala, a larger town with an array of eating establishments, grocery stores, and service businesses on which Sea Ranchers heavily rely. Bodega Bay, which is roughly comparable to Gualala in population and services, is an hour south on Highway 1. Jenner, a smaller town, is just above Bodega Bay at the mouth of the Russian River. The pristine, dramatically beautiful Pacific Coast between these towns is largely undeveloped. Although in postcard views it looks like an ideal location for a resort, the Pacific Coast of northern California has been spared large-scale resort development by its topography and weather. The terrain is fiercely rugged, the surf treacherous. The ocean waters, traveling in a southerly flow from the Gulf of Alaska, are cold year-round, and the cool, brisk winds off the Pacific make for chilly temperatures even on a sunny day in August. Winters are cool and rainy. Ocean fogs are frequent along the coastal areas. The Sea Ranch microclimate, however, enjoys the reputation of being sunnier than that of the surrounding coastline.

Sea Ranch was developed in the mid-1960s by Oceanic Properties, the real estate development arm of Castle and Cooke, a major food conglomerate based in Hawaii. Alfred Boeke, an architect and planner, was the principal in charge of the development. Boeke hired San Francisco–based landscape architect and planner Lawrence Halprin to develop a plan for the first eighteen hundred acres of the site to be developed.

Halprin's academic background included graduate work at Harvard University, where he studied design, with an emphasis on landscape design, under architects Walter Gropius and Marcel Breuer and landscape architect Christopher Tunnard. Halprin began his career in 1945 in the office of Thomas Church, the most prominent San Francisco landscape architect of his day. By the fall of 1949, Halprin had established his own practice and had developed a strong reputation for his organic garden designs for private residences. He collaborated with such notable architects as William Wurster and Joseph Esherick, and as his reputation grew, his commissions increasingly included public spaces for shopping centers, corporate office complexes, university campuses, and urban parks. By the 1960s he had developed a strong reputation for his open space designs in urban environments. However, it was his residential commissions of the late 1950s and early 1960s that would influence his approach to Sea Ranch. Greenwood Common in Berkeley, a two-and-one-half-acre site developed by William Wurster and completed in 1958 includes a half-acre common shared by twelve houses. Halprin's common, the centerpiece of the development, addressed his concern for the lack of parks and other shared amenities in suburban developments. Two years later he designed a master plan for St. Francis Square in San Francisco, a three-hundred-unit housing development where all the units face an interior communal garden, instead of the street. His use of commons would find important expression at Sea Ranch.

Halprin brought in two prominent architectural firms based in San Francisco to design the first "demonstration" buildings at Sea Ranch. The firm of Moore Lyndon Turnbull Whitaker was commissioned to design a thirty-five-acre condominium submaster plan and a ten-unit demonstration building, now known as Condominium One. The firm, whose design principals were Charles Moore, Donlyn Lyndon, William Turnbull, and Richard Whitaker, was just beginning to come to national prominence, largely based on the emerging reputation of Charles Moore. Lyndon, Turnbull, and Moore had met while studying architecture at Princeton University. Louis Kahn was an important force at Princeton during their last years there, and all have acknowledged his influence on their work.

Halprin also brought in Joseph Esherick, then practicing as Joseph Esherick and Associates. Esherick had begun his career in the office of San Francisco architect Gardner Dailey. Since 1946 he had his own practice, and at the time of his first Sea Ranch commissions, Esherick was noted primarily for residential buildings that were distinctive for their simple wood-clad forms with generous, chiefly vertical windows and intricate interior spaces. Esherick was influenced by the great wood barns of California and paid homage to their form, notably in his own residence, which he designed with his wife, also an architect, in 1950. At Sea Ranch, Esherick's first commissions were a cluster of small demonstration houses and a store, which has since been expanded by another firm to include a hotel. This building is now known as the Sea Ranch Lodge, and Esherick's houses are referred to as the Hedgerow Houses.

Halprin, MLTW, and Esherick all had notable careers in place at the time of their Sea Ranch commissions. Since the mid-1960s, their careers have all evolved to pantheon proportions. Sea Ranch would play a major role in furthering their design reputations.

The history of Sea Ranch begins, however, not with developers, planners, and designers, but with the land. This part of California was largely ignored during the Spanish, Mexican, and Russian colonial periods because of the treacherous seas and poor land access. Tiny Fort Ross, the southernmost Russian colonial outpost about fifteen miles south of the Sea Ranch site, constituted the only settlement during this early period. In 1846 Ernest Rufus, a German-born, naturalized Mexican citizen, received a land grant at this site which came to be known as "German Rancho." Another German, Frederick Hugel, raised cattle and horses, and cultivated fruits and vegetables here during the mid-nineteenth century. Most of the land that later became part of Sea Ranch remained in its pristine state. By the late 1800s, to supply construction needs in San Francisco, much of the coastal forests were clear-cut. These clear-cut areas eventually became pastures for grazing sheep. By 1906, a coastal village existed at Black Point near the present site of the Sea Ranch Lodge and Condominium One. (Today only the old barn remains.) In 1916 Walter Frick bought up the many ranches then in operation and

Twenty miles to the south of Sea Ranch along the banks of the Russian River is the town of Jenner. It is typical of the preexisting towns near Sea Ranch: Within the dramatic setting houses are clustered along steep hillsides. Retail establishments are minimal and devoted to basic needs only. A feeling of pastoral remoteness pervades these coastal communities of Sonoma County.

consolidated them under the name Del Mar Ranch. Frick planted hedgerows of cypress trees at right angles to the ocean at strategic points to serve as windbreaks for the meadows. In 1941 Del Mar Ranch was bought by the Ohlson brothers, who continued to operate a sheep ranch. In 1962, Oceanic Properties became seriously interested in the property as a potential site for a unique coastal development. Halprin, who already had a relationship with the firm and its Hawaiian properties, began a design program that served to evaluate the merit of the site for development. By 1963, agreements were in place, and in 1964, Oceanic purchased Del Mar Ranch for development as a second-home community.

The coastal expanse of Sea Ranch, though desirable for development because of its great natural beauty, had climactic limitations as the location for a traditional "beach" resort. Halprin immediately decided that the narrow, linear form of the parcel and its complex topography were not conducive to a townlike plan. Instead, he proposed clustering houses along the existing hedgerows and leaving the meadows open. The bluffs along the ocean were left undeveloped. Primary views from houses in the meadow looked across the natural landscape to the sea.

Halprin's choice to leave the coastal bluffs undeveloped was a radical idea, particularly for its time. Conventional wisdom held that the most valuable land for a coastal development was right on the coast, near the beach and the dramatic ocean views. To leave this land undeveloped was heresy to the conventional thinker. Jane Jacobs, in *The Death and Life of Great American Cities*, sheds light on the insight that fostered a different approach at Sea Ranch. Jacobs relates the story of a family that bought a parcel of land in the country on which to build a weekend home. As they dreamed about and made plans for their house, the family went to the site for weekend picnics. Their favorite picnic spot became a knoll with vistas of the countryside. Ultimately, they decided that their attraction to the knoll made it the perfect site for a house. Having carefully chosen their site, they soon commenced design and construction of their home. When the project was complete, a harsh reality set in. They had lost their treasured knoll. Their house now sat upon it, and the knoll could no longer be enjoyed and used in the manner to which they had become accustomed. They realized, too late, that they could have had a perfectly fine country house *and* their knoll, if they had only planned differently.

The coastal meadows and bluffs at Sea Ranch, kept open, could be enjoyed by all. These very important site amenities, through Halprin's plan, became community amenities. With the architecture tucked into the hedgerows, and of a scale that allowed the hedgerows to dominate, the natural landscape along the bluffs was preserved. Throughout Sea Ranch, the land held in common, particularly the commons in the coastal meadows, became a focal point of shared interest. Management of this treasured asset was expressed as a community responsibility, not a task for individual property owners looking out for their own parcels. Concern for the well-being of the Sea Ranch landscape became a galvanizing community force. That no one citizen exclusively owned a piece of the natural resource—the resource that is the very foundation of the community—both defied conventional development wisdom and cemented a bond of common interest among Sea Ranchers.

The concept of "clustering"—putting houses relatively close together to preserve open space—is integral to Halprin's plan. Four types of clusters evolved: Linear clusters are placed along the preexisting hedgerows. Cul-de-sac clusters are used at the ends of roads. Condominium sites, where the living units are part of a single large compound, are also a type of cluster. MLTW's Condominium One is the lone example of this type. The fourth type is the Walk-in Cabins, small cabins, all identical in plan, which are organically sited in a forest setting.

Along with clustering, early Sea Ranch houses found distinctive architectural expressions. MLTW's Condominium One and Esherick's Hedgerow Houses shared an approach to the Sea Ranch landscape and climate. Their eaveless shed roofs were pitched aerodynamically into the wind. This design deflected the wind and shielded the interior court of Condominium One and the rear yards of the Hedgerow Houses. The lack of eaves prevented "flutter," the incessant trembling caused by wind gusts from the Pacific. The exterior walls were clad in unpainted redwood or cedar—materials that assumed a rich, organic patina in the Sea Ranch climate. Roofing materials were wood shingle and sod which, like unpainted wood siding, gracefully reflect the passage of time. Windows, large and low to the ground, served to put the occupants right into the landscape while sheltering them from its brisk winds. These attributes, all driven by functional design considerations and appropriate design responses, came to define the "Sea Ranch style" of architecture. For all its modernist sensibilities, the Sea Ranch style was strongly influenced by the regional vernacular—the great barns and simple rural houses that predated the community.

Halprin's master plan is decentralized. Only about fifty percent of the land is privatized through sales of individual lots, and the balance of the land is held in common. Roads follow the contour of the land. Interconnections are infrequent, and most roads terminate in a cul-de-sac cluster. In no way is an urban grid suggested. This deliberately inefficient plan keeps Highway 1 as the primary thoroughfare in Sea Ranch and ensures that the private roads within the community are sparsely trafficked. Interconnected walking trails provide access to the forests, coastal bluffs, and beaches. Traditionally landscaped lawns and plantings are not permitted on private land in public view. The intent is both to preserve the indigenous landscape and to endow it with a superior status. Lawrence Halprin describes Sea Ranch as being "antisuburban," because, he says, it has very little "vest-pocket nature in it," meaning formally planted or landscaped gardens. Suburbia, he says, is

nothing but vest-pocket nature, and in this regard Sea Ranch and traditional suburbia have no resemblance. Gardens and landscaped areas are permitted at Sea Ranch but must be on private property, behind board fences, to preserve the public view of the natural landscape. Garages or board fences are required so that parked cars are similarly shielded from public view.

Land use at Sea Ranch is controlled through provisions in the "Sea Ranch Restrictions" recorded in the individual deeds to the lots. These restrictions, written by attorney Reverdy Johnson, define "restricted common areas" and "restricted private areas." Within these areas development is prohibited—no structures can be built, nor can the areas be landscaped—with only minor exceptions. Existing vegetation may be altered only with the approval of the Design Review Committee. The shielding of obviously human-altered landscape, and of cars, is integral to Sea Ranch in that it suppresses the emergence of a typical suburban landscape, even though the density and noninterconnecting, curving roads terminating in cul-de-sacs are suburban in program. Fences enforcing property lines are discouraged. In certain instances, such fences do exist in Sea Ranch. Where houses are very close together, fences are considered necessary for privacy and for screening cars, but not for demarcating property lines. An intentionally fuzzy line is desired for the boundary between individually owned and community property.

When I asked a Sea Rancher about the size of his lot, he responded that it was about a half acre, more or less, but that he really wasn't sure. He added that he wasn't sure of the exact location of his property lines. The land is left in a natural state, and commons surround three sides of his lot. From nowhere within his house could he see his neighbor's house. Where his property lines fell and how much land he personally owned were not important to him. At Sea Ranch, the physical distinction between the land shared by the community and the land constituting a private homesite is not of great importance. There is an overriding philosophical concern that the grand expanse of the natural environment at Sea Ranch not appear carved up.

The restricted common and private areas at Sea Ranch serve the dual purposes of protecting the existing landscape and suppressing the emergence of a suburban landscape, but they were not intended to ensure that the landscape of Sea Ranch, as it existed in the mid-1960s, would be frozen in time. Halprin, influenced and encouraged by the reforestation programs in Israel with which he was actively involved, began a massive tree-planting program at Sea Ranch. Over the years, thousands of trees were planted. Early photographs of Sea Ranch show the ensemble of Condominium One, the store, and the old barn standing in a treeless meadow. Today these buildings can barely be seen from Highway 1. Halprin confesses that the tree planting, though important for both aesthetic and ecological reasons, was perhaps overdone. One of the ironies of planting trees in the meadows is that the meadows and unobstructed views to the sea are what most Sea Ranchers want to see preserved. The man-made meadows, the result of early clear-cutting and grazing, if not managed and preserved, would be reclaimed by the adjacent forests over time.

The protections accorded the natural environment and the requirements imposed upon the built environment at Sea Ranch are manifested in a rather complex form through different documents. "The Sea Ranch Restrictions: A Declaration of Restrictions, Covenants and Conditions" is an officially recorded document that has legal implications for those who have purchased land in the community. It essentially functions as the community's constitution. Complementing it is the "Design Committee Rules," a document that sets forth the parliamentary and logistical procedures for the Design Review Committee and details the various restrictions and requirements imposed upon owners and their houses. Neither document includes mandates that expressly allow or forbid a specific building material or a specific style of architecture. At Sea Ranch there is no prescribed list of dos and don'ts. Instead, the Design Review Committee has the ultimate authority to oversee and evaluate a homeowner's proposal. Committee members will listen to all arguments, but their decisions are final and uncontestable.

The specific restrictions and requirements pertain not to architectural style but to the height and siting of buildings so they have a minimal impact on the natural environment and the views of adjacent properties. The Sea Ranch style, though not specifically prescribed, is articulated. Documents such as the "Sea Ranch Design Manual" are intended to familiarize owner and architect with the Sea Ranch philosophy, but none of these documents is anything like a code book. Instead of rules, the design manual contains officially endorsed design ideas and recommendations. Owners and their architects bear the responsibility for educating themselves about Sea Ranch philosophy, or they potentially face rejection of their proposals by the Design Review Committee. The reticence to establish what might be termed "design rules" or "prescribed architectural guidelines" at Sea Ranch is intentional.

Halprin referred to his design concepts at Sea Ranch as "scores" rather than "plans." This language stressed that he was not attempting to create a rigid entity, but a dynamic framework in which time and the future residents of Sea Ranch would play a role. Halprin clearly intended Sea Ranch to be a community, but what sort of community is somewhat difficult to define. Sea Ranch was not conceived as a town in any traditional sense. Nor was it a subdivision of independent estates. When I interviewed him, Halprin stated that his design for community at Sea Ranch was influenced primarily by ecosystems, the kibbutz, and the Pomo Indian culture. The Pomo Indians lived on the Sea Ranch site prior to its settlement by Europeans and were a peaceful people who sustained themselves by hunting in the coastal forests and by fishing. All three of these influences involve, to greater or lesser extents, a symbiosis between humans and the land on which they live. This symbiosis was extremely important to Halprin. For Sea Ranch he developed an elaborate "ecoscore" that began with the Jurassic period and tracked the evolution of climate, plant and animal life, and human settlement on the site. This time line defines the ecological dynamic of the land and gives perspective to the human presence upon it.

Towns, for all their compactness and efficiency, have to be artificially sustained and lack a symbiosis with the land. No room is left within them for places to grow the food and raise the livestock needed to feed their populations. Nor is there a place within towns to dispose of collective waste. These needs, along with countless others, are filled elsewhere. So a town, despite its touted efficiency, requires a much more significant area of land than that portion in which the townspeople actually live. A self-sufficient homesite that supports a house of reasonable scale with its own well, septic tank, pit or incinerator for trash, compost heap for organic garbage, family garden, and area for animals would require an amount of land roughly comparable to that of the typical rural homestead, at least a half acre. This scenario presupposes a good year-round climate with adequate rainfall, which only a small area of the planet has, and arable topsoil and minimal topographic variation over the entire parcel. The absence of any of these factors increases the amount of land required to attain self-sufficiency for the homestead.

Medieval towns in many cases needed to be completely self-sufficient. Around them were large greenbelts where the crops were grown, the slaughterhouses were located, and the dead were buried. These were the original suburbs, and they were highly undesirable as places of residence. Over time, towns and the people within them became increasingly divorced from the land that actually sustained them. The supporting lands, segregated just outside the walls of the medieval city, became an abstraction in modern times.

Although Sea Ranch was never intended to consist of self-sufficient homesites, a major aspect of the Sea Ranch concept was to get back to the land. Residents would have a symbiotic relationship with the environment, which, if not physical, could at least be spiritual. The Sea Ranch motto became "Living Lightly On The Land." For Halprin, the issues essential to Sea Ranch did not revolve around town planning, architecture, or decor, but centered on a way of life. Sea Ranch was to preserve the dominant impression of the area—the natural landscape. Charles Moore described the early architecture of Sea Ranch, particularly the MLTW condominium, "as meant neither to dominate the landscape, nor to be so dominated by it as to efface itself, but rather to come into a partnership with the landscape, to make something new that would be at home with what was there." The architecture was not meant to be transparent, and the presence of human habitation concealed. Human presence was to be coexistent with nature and was not to appear as threatening to or encroaching upon the preexisting landscape.

When Halprin developed the master plan for Sea Ranch, he brought to his firm an individual who would influence its early design and the approach of the architects who had received commissions there. This individual was Richard Reynolds, who described his profession as "ecologist," a new word in the lexicon of the early 1960s. Although not a design professional, Reynolds was consulted in the formative development of Sea Ranch. William Turnbull, particularly, acknowledges learning a great deal from him. It was Reynolds who attempted to ascertain how the development of Sea Ranch might affect the natural dynamic and what design measures could be taken to help reduce the impact of bringing to Sea Ranch what would ultimately become a relatively large number of people.

A good example of Reynolds's role concerns the sheep at Sea Ranch. Once the land had been acquired by Oceanic Properties, the developer wanted to sell off all the sheep that for decades had been grazing, and in many cases overgrazing, the coastal meadows. Reynolds, along with Turnbull, cautioned the developer that once the sheep were no longer part of the ecosystem, the grasses of the meadow would grow waist high, make the meadows unwalkable, and constitute a severe fire hazard. The only remedy would be mechanical mowing at great expense. Oceanic decided that there was no reasonable way to let the sheep continue grazing and to develop the land. The sheep were removed, and now Sea Ranchers residing in the meadows are required by the California Department of Forestry to mow a thirty-foot belt around their houses as a fire prevention measure. The grasses in the meadow are too high to walk through comfortably, so everyone sticks to the trails, many of which are mechanically mowed. Threat of brush fires is a constant concern.

About fifteen miles south of Sea Ranch is the Russian settlement of Fort Ross, founded in the early nineteenth century. The Russian Orthodox church at Fort Ross is a compelling vernacular structure that influenced the architects of Sea Ranch, particularly the principals at MLTW. Its wood roof, vertical board-and-batten siding, and interior walls of rough-hewn siding found expression in the contemporary buildings at Sea Ranch.

Other ecological concerns influenced the development program at Sea Ranch. An early little-known plan called for the timber removed for the cutting of the roads to be traded to a local lumber mill for an equal amount of sawn timber which would then be used for the construction of MLTW's condominium. The financial failure of the local mill effectively nullified this idea. This approach was based on the rural homestead, where the trees cleared for the homesite are used to build the house. The size of the house and its outbuildings is limited to the

**SHEEP RANCH**

This traditional northern California sheep ranch is a few miles inland from Bodega Bay. In the late nineteenth through the mid-twentieth centuries, sheep ranching was a common livelihood in coastal Sonoma County. This idyllic image of an artisanal relationship with the land was important for Sea Ranch.

amount of timber derived from clearing the lot so that additional forest beyond the homesite does not have to be destroyed. This approach supports the philosophy of taking no more from the landscape than it can readily afford to give up.

William Turnbull, who first became involved with Sea Ranch as a design principal at MLTW, has remained active there, garnering numerous commissions through the years. When I questioned him about the nature of the Sea

Ranch community, he responded that ensuring social interaction, creating town centers, and the like are essentially urban concerns, and are not particularly relevant to Sea Ranch because it is not an urban setting. He commented further that Sea Ranchers don't go to this second-home community for social interaction. They go there to be in a special natural environment that was developed so they could enjoy its beauty. There is some sense of community, but the primary experience is of being in a special place. Turnbull was uncomfortable describing Sea Ranch as anything other than a "settlement pattern" and added, somewhat jokingly, that if Seaside is an urban expression, then Sea Ranch is "rurban."

I concur that a word needs to be coined to describe Sea Ranch as a settlement, because nothing in the lexicon fits it, as it is neither urban nor suburban in character. It is a hybrid community. The developer's original marketing brochure describes Sea Ranch in grandiose terms as "The most unusual second-home colony ever conceived by nature and man." Subsequent marketing brochures describe it as "a unique coastal ranch." I inquired about the definition of Sea Ranch as a community to everyone knowledgeable about the place who was willing to talk to me. Universally, the initial response was a reflective pause, followed by a variety of somewhat reticent definitions: second-home community, rural settlement, a private world protected from the unworthy masses. One immediate inverse definition that many people gave is that Sea Ranch "is not a resort." Sea Ranchers do not want their community thought of as a resort, and they want to make sure that it never becomes one. There is even trepidation that some Sea Ranchers offer their homes as vacation rentals. Renters, they feel, might not understand the community, might not be considerate enough of the natural environment during their stay, or might demand resortlike amenities and commercial activities that are considered antithetical to Sea Ranch and its attributes. For many residents, a life at Sea Ranch is a privilege for which you need to accept many responsibilities, and for which ultimately you must prove yourself worthy.

Like Turnbull, Esherick has been involved with Sea Ranch since its beginning. He concurs with Turnbull that the Sea Ranch experience is not one of social interaction. He likens a weekend spent in Sea Ranch to "being alone on the frontier" and notes that before Sea Ranch was developed the site was a popular spot for camping. He remarked further that "you had confirmed what a wonderful weekend you had at Sea Ranch when you hit the gas fumes in Petaluma," a town on the northern outskirts of the Bay Area and a harbinger of your return to an urban area. For Esherick, Sea Ranch is simply a second-home community. Historically, he feels that the second home was the "big idea," the latest lifestyle trend, of the early 1960s. The post–World War II economic boom permitted the upper middle class to acquire second homes. For Esherick, Sea Ranch was part and parcel of that phenomenon, but was simply better conceived than most. On the subject of communities, Esherick elaborated that community is not defined by architecture. "Architecture does not make a community—people do. Nomadic cultures had community even though they had no substantial architecture. Nor did they even have a fixed site. Community is about shared, common interests."

Donlyn Lyndon and William Turnbull describe the importance of being at Sea Ranch in almost identical terms. Their key word is *restorative.* They both feel that most people are attracted by the beauty of the landscape at Sea Ranch and go there to get away from the city. In a Sea Ranch brochure from 1989, the presence of swimming and tennis facilities is introduced rather disdainfully: "When surveyed, Sea Ranchers agreed that access to the natural landscape far outweighs other forms of recreation. However, tennis courts, heated swimming pools, and saunas are available." Sea Ranch seems to be, more than anything else, a kind of collective Walden Pond—a retreat from conventional urbanity that proudly wears its unsullied ambience on its sleeve. There is a notion about the place that a grand social experiment by the philosophical descendants of Henry David Thoreau is at play, removed from the machinations of the complex world beyond its bounds.

Sea Ranch also impresses me as having a great deal of common ground with the Arts and Crafts movement, particularly as it was manifested in England in the early years. Arts and Crafts architecture was purposefully simple and rustic with vernacular influences. A simple life in the countryside was hailed as the superior lifestyle. There the artisan could hone his craft and produce handmade objects that were morally and physically superior to the mass-produced goods churned out in urban factories. The practitioners of the later American Arts and Crafts movement shared the attitudes of their English counterparts. Charles Keeler, in his 1904 manifesto, *The Simple Home,* describes the value of window boxes, hanging baskets of plants, roof gardens, and other methods of incorporating nature into the urban home by concluding, "But these devices are all makeshifts for the unfortunate ones who must live in the heart of a city." (Keeler lived in the newly forested Berkeley Hills and commuted to work by ferry across San Francisco Bay.) The Sea Ranch philosophy, like the attitudes of the turbulent 1960s when it was conceived, shares many of Keeler's attitudes toward the city.

The key early players at Sea Ranch could hardly be characterized as counterculture revolutionaries, but they did manage to incorporate aspects of the sociopolitical agenda of the 1960s into Sea Ranch. Middle-class values, urban life, and certainly capitalism were all called into question during this era. Conversely, the interest in communal living, particularly that based on tribal and extended family models, ecology, and a self-sufficient lifestyle, was expounded. The counterculture of the sixties began to rediscover the importance of community. If for no other reason, their rejection by and ostracism from conventional society forced them to explore an alternative community. Ultimately, most of these efforts failed, but they did succeed in triggering reevaluations of the status quo and redirected society's focus toward community, among other things. Sea Ranch, in its own way, was attempting to redirect the values of contemporary society in the 1960s.

The Sea Ranch experience proves something rather significant about the true nature of country living: the relatively close distance to one's nearest neighbor is not nearly so antithetical to the experience as the wholesale displacement of the natural realm to accommodate human presence on the land. At Sea Ranch the natural landscape comes up to the doorstep, and deer graze outside the window in a setting that is also home to jack rabbits, coveys of quail, and countless other living things. A morning walk is punctuated by chance meetings with these neighbors, as well as human ones. By contrast, in the typical automobile suburb, as Joel Garreau observes in *Edge City: Life on the New Frontier*, it is an inside joke among developers that subdivisions are named after the significant component of the natural environment destroyed in the process of building the subdivision. Hence, picturesque names like Deer Trail Estates, where there are no deer trails or deer, since the habitat was destroyed by the development that then has the audacity to market its demise.

Sea Ranch consists not only of coastal meadows converging dramatically with the ocean, though these are enough to make it a special place. Sea Ranch is a complex natural environment with hills and forests and, on its inland boundary, the Gualala River passing through on its way to the sea. As an environment for living, Sea Ranch has a character that can be roughly broken up into two primary elements, the meadows and the woods. The meadows, predominant in the coastal areas of the community, are the best-known feature. The woods are a very different environment, with houses set in stands of Bishop pine, Douglas fir, and redwoods. Some houses have views through the forest and out to the Pacific from their high perches above Highway 1. Whereas houses in the meadows seem braced to withstand the ravaging wind, houses in the woods seem embraced by a nurturing canopy. Because of the enclosure of the forest, houses in the woods are more remote and not as connected to each other as the houses in the meadows are. Rarely are you able to look out from a house set in the woods and see much of a neighboring house, though one may be very close by. The woods offer the greatest degree of seclusion, both real and perceived, within Sea Ranch.

As you approach Sea Ranch, it reveals itself in stages rather than all at once, which might seem unusual for such a dramatic and well-known place. As you drive north from Bodega Bay, you repeatedly encounter hairpin turns and spectacular ocean views. The views are glimpses of a world that possesses a fantastical dramatic beauty, while the hairpin turns are an immediate and nagging distraction. You experience an emotional rollercoaster as the oncoming landscape and seascape bare themselves majestically, then you get an adrenaline aftertaste as you focus on maneuvering your car through the next precipitous turn and avoiding an over-the-cliff merger with the sublime inspiration of only a few seconds ago.

Your arrival at Sea Ranch just north of Stewart's Point is not clearly demarcated in spite of the sign at the southern boundary. None of the community's residences front Highway 1. There are no notable landmarks or monuments along the way, or a town center, to symbolize your arrival at a specific place of importance. In fact, much of Sea Ranch's architecture is not even visible from the slalom track that is Highway 1. Sea Ranch is, more than anything else, part of the continuum of the remarkably dramatic landscape through which you've been weaving precariously for the past hour. When you reach the Gualala River at the north end of Sea Ranch and cross over it into the town of Gualala, it is obvious that the drama of nature's magnificence has been completely interrupted by something man-made—the mundanity of strip centers and filling stations. Beneath these more recent "achievements," you get the sense of what was once a quaint little coastal town.

Seen from Highway 1, Sea Ranch, as a built environment, is a rather subtle manifestation. You sense this was intended. The community doesn't open up to you right away, and this too, I think, if not intentional, is tolerated as the by-product of some greater purpose. Like the complex topography of its site, Sea Ranch takes a good deal of exploration and investigation before you can establish a sense of belonging and gain a good grasp of the "rules." There are many layers to the private realm of Sea Ranch. First, the entire community is private. If you are not a homeowner, or a guest of one, you have no legal right to be here. Indeed, a security force is present to ensure the community's privacy. Even if you are a homeowner—and therefore what is private to everybody else is your public realm—individually owned property within this private world is off-limits to you just as it would be in any other community. But this property has no clear boundary. When you are in Sea Ranch and see signs that say "Private Property/No Trespassing," you pause to reflect whether this applies to you. This is the kind of place where your first encounter is greatly enhanced if you are introduced by an insider, like the first excursion to a new club in which you have just been made a member. Initial misgivings of belonging are quickly overcome by a strong sense of being in a special place far away from everything associated with an ordinary existence.

As of this writing, all of the Sea Ranch homesites have been sold by the developer. Resales of existing lots and houses constitute the only sales activity. Slightly over half the lots, of which there are a total of 2,305, have been developed. According to Ted Smith, Director of Planning and Design at Sea Ranch, the Design Review Committee approves about eighty new houses per year. At this rate, Sea Ranch will not be "built out" for another fifteen years.

The entire Sea Ranch parcel originally included about fifty-three hundred acres, and Halprin was directly involved in the planning for only the first eighteen hundred. Sixteen hundred acres in the woods were subsequently sold to Travelers Insurance. Travelers, in turn, sold the northern portion to Gualala Redwoods, a timber company engaged in the progressive approach of selective cutting and long-term forest management, rather than clear-cutting. The Sea Ranch Association repurchased from Travelers a central parcel of three hundred acres, and a private individual bought two hundred twenty acres at the south end and used it as a setting for a single large house that prominently surveys the Pacific. The balance of Sea Ranch, about sixty percent of what was ultimately platted and sold off, was planned by in-house staff, following approximately the design principles initiated by Halprin in the 1960s. Although no deliberate attempt was made to undermine Halprin's concepts, changes were readily made to accommodate practical and financial concerns. As a result, the character of the community was affected. Most of the differences can be readily seen on a plat map.

On the northern half of Sea Ranch, the platting is more typical of that of an automobile suburb, and the lots tend to encroach more on the coastal bluffs. The desire for a central sewer system was a major influence. To accommodate the system, the lots are lined up and the organic flow of houses is compromised by the imposition of a more urban order. The typical lot is also smaller on the north side, but the houses built on these smaller lots are in many cases larger. On lots the size of the ones Esherick placed his diminutive Hedgerow Houses came newer houses with the scale of four- or five-bedroom suburban ranch homes. The form of the suburban ranch home also tends to predominate in the northern half of Sea Ranch. There seems to be a strong sentiment at Sea Ranch that, as more of the land is built upon, owners and/or their architects should increasingly be held in check by design review. In the February 1993 *Progressive Architecture*, Donlyn Lyndon, who served for many years on the Sea Ranch Design Review Committee, lamented that "even design review cannot bring a cadaver to life." Design review is limited by what homeowners submit. Hampered primarily by a slow build-out, the potentially pervasive influence of the early demonstration buildings—Condominium One and the Hedgerow Houses—never reached critical mass. A second condominium building was built, but it shares few attributes with the remarkable and landmark first one. Esherick faults the propensity for telephone real estate sales, for reducing the influence of the Hedgerow Houses as prototypes. The siting and clustering concepts were too complex to explain verbally. They really needed to be seen by potential purchasers to encourage widespread emulation within the community. These factors, along with other developments, resulted in the gradual emergence of a more typically suburban form of architecture embedded in a more suburban community plan than the Sea Ranch of Halprin's original concept.

As the community has built out, a downside to Halprin's decentralized plan for Sea Ranch has emerged: life in the community is dependent upon the automobile. The walking trails are interconnected and always close by, but distances are great, and all practical errands require a car. With the dearth of retail services in Sea Ranch, residents have to go to Stewart's Point on the south end or Gualala on the north end for provisions. Sea Ranchers commonly refer to such errands as "going into town." Janann Strand, a longtime Sea Ranch resident, expresses this in very plausible terms: "Coming up to Sea Ranch is a lot like camping. You have to be prepared." Getting provisions is not the only need for a car. Regardless of one's location within the community, going to the beach, to the recreational facilities, to the stables, or to any number of the many points of interest in this long, linear community requires a car. Those who desire the experience that Sea Ranch provides should expect to assume responsibility for getting around in the remoteness. Yet Sea Ranchers have made an effort to leave urbanity behind and commune with nature, and it is unfortunate to have to rely so much on the automobile while in Sea Ranch. The noise, pollution, and visual presence of the automobile seem out of place. Some recognition of the automobile as antithetical to Sea Ranch is evident in the requirement that cars be garaged or screened from public view by a board fence. All Sea Ranchers and visitors must have permit stickers for their

**THE DEVELOPMENT**

Louisiana artist Douglas Bourgeois's

painting, *The Development*, graphically

protests the suburbanization of the

American rural landscape.

cars. Cars without them are subject to booting. The roads within the community are not public, but private. Sea Ranchers clearly want to control the number of cars in their community and hide the ones that are there. Although their reasons are justified, my only criticism is that dependence on the automobile has never been addressed as a planning issue.

Dependence on the automobile within Sea Ranch could be mitigated somewhat by the plans for Sea Ranch Village, a small complex offering about four thousand square feet of leasable retail space. It is a much-needed addition to the community which shouldn't interfere with its nonurban character. This development would go a long way toward establishing a town center for Sea Ranch. There is some resistance to it among residents, however. They mostly fear that it would attract more people from outside the community. They also suspect that this small breach could open a floodgate of commercial development which would turn the quiet community into a full-fledged resort. I see why these fears are present, particularly since rampant growth in California has dramatically changed the context and character of virtually everyone's public domain. Retrenchment is probably not the answer, though. Sea Ranch Village would put needed retail services within walking or biking distance for a significant number of Sea Ranchers and would shorten car trips for others.

As Sea Ranch has matured as a community, land prices have risen steadily, and resale prices of existing homes have climbed dramatically, too. Becoming a member of the Sea Ranch community is not as simple as it was in the late 1960s and early 1970s, when weekend visitors, intoxicated with the serene beauty of the coast, would impulsively purchase land. Many lots could be purchased for only a few thousand dollars each. A down payment of a few hundred dollars and land payments that slightly exceeded the monthly utility bill made the prospect of a second home at Sea Ranch attainable for anyone of middle-class means. This is no longer the case. Only the affluent can purchase a home or lot in Sea Ranch. New members of the Sea Ranch community share at least one thing: their wealth.

For Lawrence Halprin, diversity was intrinsic to the principle of Sea Ranch. The goal of Sea Ranch, he says, was to have "a great diversity of people in their interests, backgrounds, and, hopefully, incomes." He concedes that Sea Ranch has not been as successful in realizing this as he had hoped. But, he concludes, "We try." At least, the desire for diversity is there. Halprin points out that Sea Ranch was never intended to be anything like 17-Mile Drive in Carmel—a seventeen-mile stretch of beautiful coastline near Carmel, interspersed with villas in sylvan settings, adjacent to some of the world's most renowned golf courses. A structure resembling a toll booth marks the beginning of the drive. Here commoners are charged a fee for the privilege of making the drive and gawking at the auspicious wealth of the local gentry. It is a car-tour version of "Lifestyles of the Rich and Famous." I have to concur with Halprin: regardless of how monolithically affluent Sea Ranch may become, it will never be comparable to 17-Mile Drive.

Along with the changes in the character of Sea Ranch, there were devastating financial setbacks in the 1970s. In 1972, through the California initiative process, environmental groups placed Proposition 20, the Coastal Initiative, on the ballot. This proposition sought to block further private development of the California coast and set up a regulatory body to manage and provide public access to the state's coastal resources. Passage of Proposition 20 brought the continued development of Sea Ranch to a halt. The proposition was also psychologically hurtful to Sea Ranch. A community that had always looked on itself as environmentally conscious was now cast in the public view as part of the then-prevalent trend of privatizing the California coast for the benefit of the state's most affluent citizens while denying public access to this most notable natural asset.

Subsequent legislation in 1976 established the California Coastal Commission as the state's coastal regulatory body. By 1980, negotiations between The Sea Ranch Association and the commission resulted in a set of compromises enacted into the Bane Bill which allowed continued development. The Bane Bill required that the developer reduce the number of homesites from 3,000 to 2,305, ensure public access to the beach at prescribed intervals within the community, and provide sites for low-income housing. The reduction in density was facilitated by the conversion of future condominium sites to single-family homesites and/or commons. The final impact of the Coastal Initiative tended toward the negative for Sea Ranch. The conversion of potential condominium sites prevented this type of housing cluster from contributing to the community as Condominium One had. The ecological concerns integral to the Sea Ranch ideal were considered insignificant in the public mind when measured against the coastal privatization and exclusivity of the community. Although the presence of residents receiving public relief and living in "worker housing" theoretically enhances the socioeconomic diversity at Sea Ranch, I've seen no evidence that these residents are genuinely considered to be part of the Sea Ranch community. Public access to the coast, not just within Sea Ranch but throughout the state, is the one paramount goal that the initiative achieved. It is important symbolically and should have existed all along. Within Sea Ranch this access was delivered in a compatible and reasonable manner that has not, in my view, negatively impacted the community significantly.

The lack of building activity and the uncertainty of the community's future for such an extended period had great financial repercussions on Oceanic Properties (now Oceanic California, Inc.). By the 1980s Oceanic had finally sold the currently platted, improved property and had decided to sell its outstanding holdings, which the company viewed as not very lucrative for development, to Travelers Insurance. The Sea Ranch Association, a homeowner-supported corporation, is now in charge of managing the community and keeping in place the Design Review Process. Thirty years after it all began, Sea Ranch is controlled exclusively by Sea Ranchers and the institutions they put in place to govern it.

The governance of Sea Ranch and the community debates over major issues have at times assumed gothic proportions. Allegations and insinuations have been flung from homeowner to homeowner, from homeowners to The Sea Ranch Association, and in prior days from The Sea Ranch Association to Oceanic Properties. There have been spirited arguments, massive letter writing campaigns, and even ersatz coup attempts. Sea Ranch resident Janann Strand describes these adventures as "engaging in constructive mischief." Some may have expected the decision-making process in such a utopian-minded community to be much less contentious and more agreeable. Yet what actually occurs at Sea Ranch is at the center of self-government and democracy—a vortex of debate and varied opinion from which, it is hoped, some reasoned collective decision ultimately springs.

Time has a way of dampening utopian enthusiasm, and particularly through the trying times of the 1970s, the Sea Ranch ideal tended to get buried beneath other problems and concerns. As the community ultimately prevailed through this, a desire to rekindle the spirit of the early days has begun to emerge. In the mid-1980s the community went through some reassessments. Many of the early design principals and administrators were joined by new participants, architect Donald MacDonald and landscape architect and planner Hideo Sasaki, and in an effort overseen by Jack Cosner, then administrator of the Design Review Committee, they reviewed the successes and failures of Sea Ranch. Fresh ideas and numerous proposals were made to help ensure the future viability of the community. This formalized administrative effort has been complemented in recent years by other, back-to-the-roots endeavors. Lawrence Halprin has conducted recent workshops in which Sea Ranchers discuss their attraction to the community and how they can better contribute to the well-being of Sea Ranch. These kinds of efforts offer evidence that early goals that might have gotten sidetracked along the way are being rediscovered and that the Sea Ranch ideal is finding continued expression.

With the original developer out of the picture, all the homesites in private ownership, and many impediments in its evolution surmounted, Sea Ranch has reached a point of maturity. Its early buildings have become architectural landmarks of their period. In 1991, Condominium One received the prestigious 25 Year Award from the national chapter of the American Institute of Architects. The Sea Ranch style has become a commonly acknowledged suburban architectural style. It is even mentioned in Virginia and Lee McAlester's 1984 book, *A Field Guide to American Houses*, as the "shed style" attributed to the influences of Charles Moore, a prominent Sea Ranch architect, and to Robert Venturi, who was not, but who in the 1960s was revisiting the shingle style on the East Coast.

As a community type, Sea Ranch is unique. Its focus on the natural environment as the primary determinant for the built environment and its key role in the evolution of what has come to be known as ecological or environmentally sensitive design are significant achievements. Residents who appreciate nature and understand their role as stewards of the land are far more vigilant than some of the bureaucracies put in place to preserve the environment. The greatest travesties against nature that we commit are invariably in remote places where no one lives to bear witness to nature's demise. But because of our propensity to transform the natural environment to accommodate the human population, even a small one, our societal attitude has been to stay off the land entirely. Those who live in the countryside don't typically want more people living there because this invariably leads to a suburbanization of the natural landscape. Sea Ranch offers the promise that ecologically sensitive land management and preservation of the natural environment are compatible with rural community living. Sea Ranch demonstrates that those who prefer the country to the city need not sacrifice community and live a hermetic life. Even at low densities in a nonurban setting, shared purpose and common experiences in a public realm can be a normal part of life.

Some observers may feel that Sea Ranch does not offer enough community for them. Social interaction as it is found in the small-town experience may not be as readily available at Sea Ranch. The dearth of retail businesses within the community denies the basic requirements for sustaining a human population and the opportunities for casual social interaction. But these contemporary judgments fail to give proper historical perspective to what was accomplished in the mid-1960s.

Looking back to the decade before Sea Ranch for prominent examples of modern architecture that promoted the dynamic interaction of human habitat and nature, there is Philip Johnson's Glass House in Connecticut, Mies van der Rohe's Farnsworth House in Illinois, and Richard Neutra's Desert House in Arizona. All these elegant, sculptural works have the thinnest, most transparent membrane possible between humans and nature. But, as Vincent Scully has commented, specifically about Johnson's Glass House, "You cannot build community with this architecture." To place anything other than nature in proximity to the Glass House is to defile it. This kind of architecture, as numerous critics have observed, exists only as a sculptural object in space. It does not contribute to any pattern in the sense that Christopher Alexander so eloquently expressed.

Sea Ranch developed an architecture that connected mankind and nature dynamically and provided for community. This was not a small achievement. At a time when community was taken for granted, or worse yet considered dispensable, Sea Ranch addressed community and, in this regard, deserves acknowledgment as an early component of the renewed interest in community that we now experience. In hindsight, its embrace of community seems ancillary, but then this is characteristic of many awakenings. They start small and grow, but the places where they start ultimately become extremely important.

Sea Ranch offers an environment at a density comparable to that of automobile suburbia, but is far more compelling and has a far greater shared purpose among its residents. It is what automobile suburbia had the potential to be, but isn't.

The Sea Ranch environment offers much

more than a dramatic coastline and royal

blue expanse of ocean. Trails have been

cut through hilly forests. The one on the

opposite page winds to The Hot Spot, a

picnic area along the Gualala River.

There are views through trees wrapped in a veil of early morning fog—a setting typical of houses in the woods. Coastal meadows are home to wildflowers and other vegetation. Sea Ranch is firmly anchored in its natural beauty. The built environment is ancillary, physically and conceptually.

SEA RANCH FROM MOONRAKER ROAD

Much of the community of Sea Ranch can be seen from this elevated vantage point along Moonraker Road. The dominant impression is of sea, hills, forest, and sky, but within the landscape are actually hundreds of houses.

What would ultimately come to be known as the "Sea Ranch style" of architecture was influenced by these early buildings with their vertical board siding and the surrounding rustic wood fences.

## RUINS OF DEL MAR RANCH

The ruins of Del Mar Ranch, the ranch that stood on the property before the building of Sea Ranch, are haunting reminders of the history of human habitation on the land. These structures include the old barn near the Sea Ranch Lodge and a sheepherder's cabin known as "One-Eyed Jack's" adjacent to the picnic area and playground near the physical center of the community.

The old Del Mar schoolhouse, a country schoolhouse where children growing up on the ranch were educated, is near Highway 1 on the north side of the community.

Del Mar schoolhouse, viewed from Highway 1, reveals its relationship with a contemporary Sea Ranch residence on a coastal bluff in the distance.

## CONDOMINIUM ONE

Anchored on an imposing bluff overlooking the Pacific is the condominium compound designed by the San Francisco firm of Moore, Lyndon, Turnbull, and Whitaker, known as Condominium One. Marvin Buchanan and Ed Allen also made significant contributions to its design. The compound was described in Moore, Allen, and Lyndon's 1974 book *The Place of Houses:* "At once castle, compound, and promontory, it is a concentration of dwellings bunched together in the teeth of the wind."

The shed roof follows the contour of the land and deflects the brisk Pacific winds. Within the fortresslike walls are parking structures, a landscaped courtyard with a deck, and ten condominium units, variations on a twenty-four-foot module, all designed and oriented to capture sun and shield wind. Although Condominium One is essentially a modernist design, the overall statement incorporates vernacular counterpoints: weathered, vertical board walls, heavy timber framing, and a scale evocative of the large barns found in this part of northern California.

## FRAMING DETAIL

Condominium One is not a typical balloon frame with two-by-fours set sixteen inches on center, but consists of exposed, heavy timber framing. The architects appreciated the structural beauty of this type of construction, frequently found in old barns in the region, so they left the construction framing exposed as a visual element within the interiors of the condominium units.

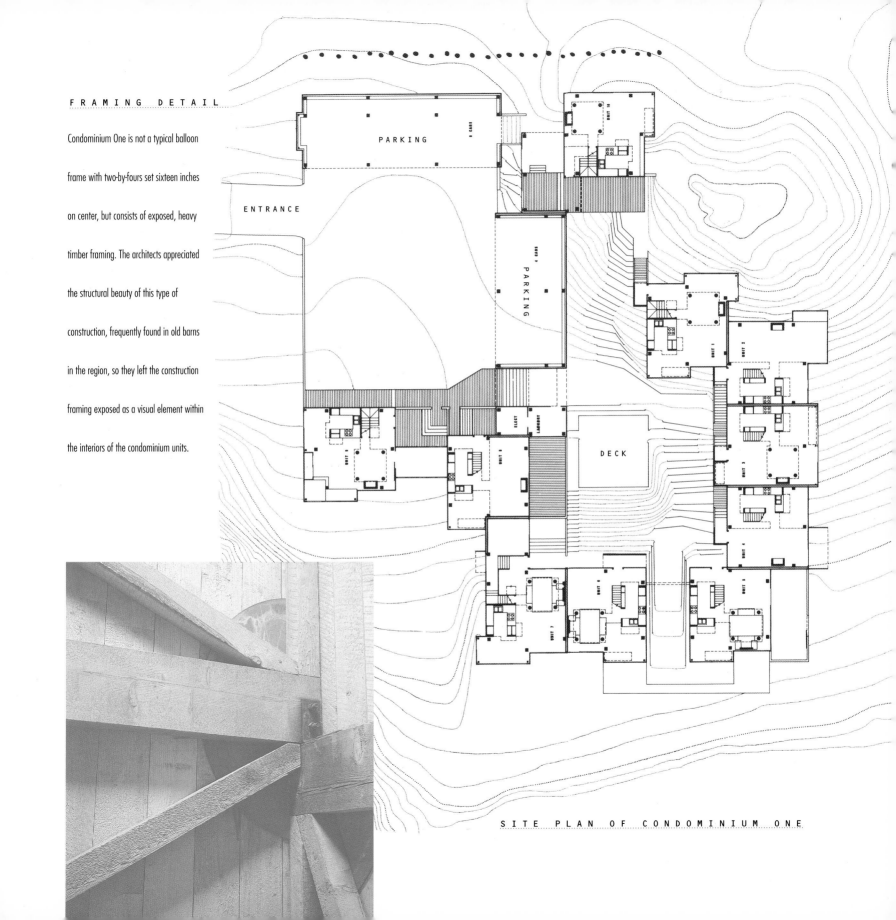

PARKING

ENTRANCE

PARKING

DECK

SITE PLAN OF CONDOMINIUM ONE

## MEADOW AT BLACK POINT BEACH

This panoramic vista from Black Point takes in houses clustered along hedgerows of Monterey cypress on both sides of the coastal meadows. The houses look obliquely across the meadow to the sea. To the right are Joseph Esherick's Hedgerow Houses. Walking trails hug the bluff. Stairs provide access to Black Point Beach at two intervals. In the background are the coastal hills covered with redwoods, Douglas fir, and Bishop pine. Here and there houses peek out of the woods, catching dramatic ocean views.

An early demonstration house designed in 1965 by Joseph Esherick and Associates emerges from the meadow overlooking Black Point Beach. It is one house in a cul-de-sac cluster of six at the end of Black Point Reach. These houses, connected at the rear by a continuous board fence, have come to be known as the Hedgerow Houses. Along with MLTW's Condominium One, these simple houses came to define the Sea Ranch style: The siding of wood shingles or vertical redwood boards is left unpainted. The shed roofs either are angled into the wind or follow the topographic flow, and are eaveless to prevent wind flutter. Generous windows positioned low in the walls bring the dramatic views of the natural landscape into the interiors.

On the left side of the Sea Ranch Lodge is the portion of the original building designed by Joseph Esherick and Associates and first known as the

Sea Ranch store. Its prototype was the country general store—an appropriate concept—but the business could not sustain itself financially. The

arcade to the right is an addition by another firm. The lodge contains a post office, a souvenir shop (the only remnant of the Sea Ranch store), a bar,

a restaurant, and a real estate office. A small hotel is next door. The large graphic of a stylized ram's head above the entry, designed by Barbara

Stauffacher, has become the symbol of Sea Ranch. It is used on sales brochures, parking permit stickers, maps, and community newsletters.

## VERDANT VIEW BUSINESS PARK

The newer of two commercial buildings houses design and real estate offices and other nonretail businesses at Verdant View off Annapolis Road. This area of Sea Ranch, well removed from the coastal areas, was allocated for what were termed "business parks."

Adjacent to the commercial area is an airstrip with hangers for private planes, designed by architect Dan Levin. Nonresidential land use is decentralized at Sea Ranch. The lodge

and hotel are at the south end of the coast. The airstrip, administration, and commercial buildings are in the hills off Annapolis Road. The chapel and fire station are off Highway 1 near the physical center of the community. One rec center is at the south coast, and the other is near the middle of the coast, close to the equestrian facility. A golf course and pro shop are at the extreme north of the community.

## OLD BARN, LODGE, AND CONDOMINIUM ONE

A single panoramic view encompasses the old Sea Ranch barn, standing alone in the middle of the meadow; Sea Ranch Lodge, to the left, comprising the original Sea Ranch store by Joseph Esherick and Associates and a hotel addition by another firm; and MLTW's Condominium One, at the extreme right, behind a screen of planted cypress trees.

## NORTH REC CENTER

There are two recreational centers at Sea Ranch. The older, and smaller, one is known as the Moonraker Rec Center and dates from

1966. The newer one, shown here, was designed in 1969 and is called the North Rec Center. It is located near the physical center of

Sea Ranch. Both were a collaboration between the architectural firm of MLTW and Lawrence Halprin. The design incorporates berms that

serve as windbreaks and a "wind-wall." The central building is sited to shield the heated swimming pool from the wind. The wind-wall

segregates the tennis courts from the pool area and contains three saunas and changing and shower facilities. The rec centers are the

primary architectural elements that provide a public forum for Sea Ranchers.

## SEA RANCH BEACHES

Along with the hiking trails, the

beaches at Sea Ranch are the

community's most populated places.

Although the wind and the water are

always cool, Sea Ranchers find a

variety of ways to enjoy the beaches.

## SEA RANCH STABLES AND EQUESTRIAN FACILITY

Along Highway 1, near the North Rec Center, are the Sea Ranch Stables and Equestrian Facility. Participating Sea Ranchers may stable their horses in facilities provided by The Sea Ranch

Association. Many Sea Ranch trails are allocated for horseback riding. The presence of these stables in the community further enhances the notion of Sea Ranch as being ranchlike not only in

ambience but in actuality.

## MEADOW AT WALK ON BEACH

Some Sea Ranchers may disapprove of this growing cluster of houses on the meadow at Walk On Beach. Four roughly parallel roads reach into the meadow and access lots which, when fully developed, will fill the meadow with a total of about twice the number of houses seen here. The meadow at Walk On Beach is typical of the platting in the northern half of Sea Ranch. The pristine landscape of the meadow is undeniably being altered, but the effect of a rustic village is not unappealing. Even though the density of the cluster approaches that of automobile suburbia, this vista shows how the Sea Ranch landscape program suppresses the formation of a typical suburban expression: formal garden landscaping, parked cars, and property line fences are not allowed, and a substantial common area is preserved as open space.

## SEA RANCH CHAPEL

Reminiscent of Eero Saarinen's John F. Kennedy International Airport Terminal and Antonio Gaudí's Casa Mila in Barcelona, the Sea Ranch Chapel was designed by James Hubbell, an artist from Santa Ysabel, California, and completed in 1985. It sits, in a curious juxtaposition, adjacent to the North Fire Station along Highway 1. Not large enough for traditional religious services, the nondenominational chapel is intended for either an individual or a small group.

Consistent with other attributes of Sea Ranch, the chapel is more fitting for an individual to use in his or her own way than for regularly held group denominational worship.

REDWOOD RISE

MADRONE MEADOW

The roads of Sea Ranch are never considered as streets in the urban sense. They provide vehicular access to the houses, and that is the end of their similarity to conventional streets. The meandering roads tend to follow the topography. Their names, such as Wild Moor Reach and Leeward Road, suggest landmarks in, or country trails through, the wilderness. The intersection of Madrone Meadow and Redwood Rise is marked by this typical road sign—a rough-sawn, whitewashed, four-by-four finished off with an angle cut echoing the shed roofs of Sea Ranch houses. The letters are simple stenciled characters. This signage is a fine example of how the community maintains the overall ambience of being in the country.

The trails of Sea Ranch follow organic routes, just as the roads do, though they connect to other trails or to roadways. Heavily traveled trails are established by foot trampling, and less used trails, like this one, by a mowed path. At chosen intervals, low signs mark the trail and indicate the kinds of transport allowed on it. A few trails allow bicycles, but none permit motorized trail bikes or three-wheelers.

One of the most common opportunities for casual social interaction in Sea Ranch exists along the many miles of hiking trails. Interaction usually is limited to a simple hello or a polite nod. Most Sea Ranchers are not walking the trails to find sociability but, rather, to experience nature. This motive establishes a fairly rigid parameter for how much and what kinds of social interaction will reasonably, and naturally, occur.

50 hardworking families belong to this garden. Visitors are welcome to look but not pick. If you would like to join us next year, call 785-2357 or ▮▮▮▮▮▮▮▮

## P O S H   S Q U A S H   G A R D E N

One of the best examples of community at Sea Ranch is the community garden—the "Posh Squash Garden." Families volunteer to work a minimum of three hours per week in order to participate. By working the minimum hours, Sea Ranchers can pick the vegetables they need for their family's use. Those who don't help with the work are free to admire the garden, but can't pick anything. A desktop-published newsletter, *The Compost Heap*, informs participants about the membership list, the watering schedule, and the like. The leadership hierarchy begins with the Dictator—Mother Nature, and follows with the Coordinator, essentially the head person; the Day Leaders, who supervise volunteers; and the Support Services, which include a range of jobs from being in charge of producing the newsletter to repairing irrigation equipment.

Participating in the community garden involves commitment, responsibility, and sharing. It is one place within the community where Sea Ranchers are assured, during daylight hours, to find their neighbors congregating with a shared purpose. Ironically, the community garden is on land adjacent to Sea Ranch and is technically not a part of it. This is due to the requirement that formally planted areas must be fenced—only the natural environment can be publicly visible—and fences must meet the approval of the Design Review Committee. A simple fence of vertical boards would be acceptable, but enclosing an area as large as this vegetable garden was too costly for a volunteer group with nominal revenue.

## WALK-IN CABINS

Among the most romantic, and fully conceived, housing clusters at Sea Ranch are the walk-in cabins designed by Obie Bowman. They

are so named because they are clustered in the woods and must be reached on foot from the adjacent parking areas. This compelling

arrangement of diminutive cabins tucked away in a pristine forest was Bowman's first Sea Ranch project. He came to Sea Ranch from

southern California after becoming disillusioned with working at a large firm that designed shopping strips which "ate up the land." He

decided to part company with urban life, a radical move for an architect, and has since operated a small design office at Sea Ranch.

**SITE PLAN**

The walk-in cabins are simple and rather unremarkable structures. Their setting and sensitive, organic siting make them one of the greatest achievements at Sea Ranch.

The site plan shows how the fifteen walk-in cabins are clustered. The gravel road that winds back into the cluster is for loading and unloading only. Vehicles are parked in the parallel spaces on the main road.

## BOOMERANG HOUSE

In striking contrast to Windhover, this house, also designed by Obie Bowman in the

 mid-1980s, is excavated so that its sod roof becomes an extension of the meadow.

More than perhaps any other building at Sea Ranch, this structure, informally known as

the "boomerang house," seeks to be a marriage between building and land, rather than,

as Charles Moore termed Sea Ranch architecture, a limited partnership between

building and land.


Unlike the area of Sea Ranch on the south end platted according to Halprin's hedgerow

clustering concept, this area of Sea Ranch has lots that encroach farther into the meadow.

Bowman sought to camouflage his house in an effort to ensure that the natural

environment remain the dominant impression.

## WINDHOVER

Designed by Obie Bowman in the late

1980s, Windhover is distinctive for the

massive tree-trunk columns on its front

porch. The tree-trunk columns, in a

contrived naiveté, mimic the living trunks

behind them. The gable is ornamented

with a clocklike circle of vents. Because

the house is set against a tall hedgerow,

which serves as a background, it is able

to achieve a significant verticality without

dominating the natural environment.

## BARN HOUSES

William Turnbull in collaboration with Charles Moore designed a series of "barn houses." This

simple design was offered by the developer as a generic plan for anyone lacking the interest or

resources to hire an architect and go through the design approval process. The first house was

designed in 1967; by 1972 seventeen had been built with minor variations. Their design

represents an evolution from the Sea Ranch style of modernist design tempered by the vernacular

to outright vernacular-inspired architecture. Some of the most natural-looking buildings at

Sea Ranch, the barn houses genuinely look as though they belong on the land. They did

not prove to be trendsetters, however. Later architecture at Sea Ranch has tended to be

more massive in scale and suburban in form.

## LYNDON–WINGWALL HOUSE

Donlyn Lyndon designed this house and studio as a second home for himself and his wife, Alice Wingwall. Although completed in January 1993, it is strongly evocative of the principles that went into the early Sea Ranch buildings—Condominium One, for which Lyndon was a design principal, and Esherick's Hedgerow Houses. It is eloquent evidence of the timelessness and appropriateness of this approach to design at Sea Ranch.

## SHINEFIELD HOUSE

In 1971 Charles Moore and Dmitri Vedensky designed the Shinefield house, named after the family who commissioned it. Set deep into the bluff of the ocean meadow and shielded by berms behind and planted cypresses on the left, it merges with the landscape.

## LIFTING FOG

The dynamics of weather and

atmosphere are always apparent at Sea

Ranch. Ocean fog encroaches in the

evening and lifts dramatically the

following morning. As the forest

emerges from the dispersing fog, a

feeling of quiet melancholy is about to

give way to the exuberance and much

anticipated warmth of morning sunshine.

## WORKER HOUSING

Low-income, government-subsidized housing exists within Sea Ranch as a result of the

Bane Bill, legislation that ended the moratorium on coastal development in California in

1980. Generally referred to as "worker housing," these buildings were designed by

William Turnbull in the vernacular language. Of the two buildings seen here, the one on the

right is a literal adaptation of a sharecropper's cabin used for rural housing in the South.

## CHARLES MOORE, CONDOMINIUM ONE, UNIT 9

From the completion of Condominium One until his death in December 1993, Unit Nine was the place of retreat for architect Charles Moore. He spent as much time here as his career would allow, about two months a year. Moore described Sea Ranch as his "Mother Earth," a sanctuary where he went to rekindle his energy and spirit. Throughout his heralded career, Moore made pilgrimages to Sea Ranch from a succession of primary residences, in Berkeley, New Haven, Los Angeles, and Austin, Texas.

Moore's "large furniture" functions as kitchen, stair, bath, and sleeping loft (see axonometric drawing). This element, common to all the condominium units, is freestanding within the twenty-four-foot cube of the rough-sawn, heavy-timber structure. It is of painted, smooth wood which contrasts dramatically with the rough, unfinished box surrounding it.

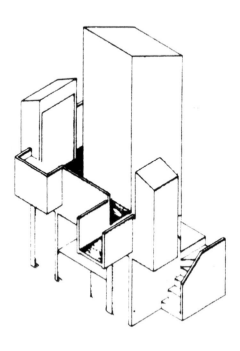

The checkerboard pattern of the kitchen was inspired both by Walter Chatham's house in Seaside and by Katsura Villa in Kyoto, the seventeenth century palace built as the country house for Prince Toshihito. Above the kitchen is an Indian painting depicting dancing goddesses. The bath, located above the kitchen, serves as the base for a sleeping loft accessed by a vertical stair. In the right foreground is the headboard of a settee adorned with a Victorian soffit vent. In the background on the left is the dining area. On its far wall is an Indian drawing, a gift from architect Charles Correa. Below it is the architectural model of a now-demolished theater in Houston. The two grand Balinese cane chairs create a cozy area that looks out to the sitting bays and ocean view.

Beneath the main sleeping loft, which rests on four massive wooden poles, is a metal firebox that sits on a slate hearth. Behind it is a section from a fourteenth century Spanish ceiling acquired at an estate sale at William Randolph Hearst's San Simeon and adorned with abalone shells from the Sea Ranch vicinity and carved wood animals from Mexico.

A window seat designed for relaxation and contemplation looks out to the Pacific surf.

The sleeping loft, another example of large furniture, is arranged for sleeping and working. The bedside table is home to an arrangement of functional clay pottery in a bovine motif by Moore's nephew, Steven Weingarten. The sleeping loft is lit by a skylight whose light is directed and softened by a canvas surround. Canvas shades can be lowered to achieve more privacy and create a tentlike room which Moore described as having "a sexy Rudolph Valentino aura."

The view from the sleeping-loft desk emphasizes the volumetric space above the main living area.

At the landing of the stair to the sleeping loft is a vertical bookcase whose top shelves are for books and whose bottom shelves are for linens.

A solarium adjacent to the main floor can be closed off by a barn door. In his later years, Moore had difficulty climbing the stairs to access the bath and sleeping areas, so he designed within the solarium a self-contained module with an additional bed and bath. Behind the large door is a Murphy bed. To the right is a half bath, and at the end of the short corridor on the left is a shower stall—a tidy arrangement that requires no more room than a typical small bath.

Moore's Unit Nine is a complex, compact space filled with eclectic treasures, sometimes whimsical but always meaningful, collected over a lifetime. During Moore's life, this residence continued to evolve and reflected the many transitions of his celebrated career.

CONDOMINIUM ONE,
UNIT 9
**OWNER** *Charles Moore*
**ARCHITECT** *MLTW*
**DATE** *Completed in 1965*
**CONTRACTOR** *Matt Sylvia,*
*Matthew Sylvia Construction Co.*

## TEEL HOUSE

The Teel house is the second home of San Franciscans Jeffrey and Brenda Teel. Jeffrey Teel, an architect, is a principal at the firm of Robinson Mills Williams. He designed the house in 1984, and construction was completed in the spring of 1986. Without hedging, Teel describes himself as a modernist. He did not wish to deviate from the aesthetics of the Sea Ranch style, but wanted to create a house that would be considered a classic within that style. He felt that architectural experimentation could be realized in aspects of the design other than in exterior appearance. The house is relatively small, at 1,150 square feet, not counting the garage and deck.

The twilight veiw is of the front of the house, which faces the road. The board fence shields a woodpile and parking for one car and forms an entry corral. The understated entry is in the central niche on the ground floor.

The back of the house looks to the northeast across the gently sloping meadow on which it is sited. The siding of clear heart redwood has a natural finish, the only treatment being a preservative.

The main living area of the house is a grand loft on the second floor, accessed by stairs behind the fireplace. A wedge-shaped, inverted window bay allows entrants to view the space above and permits greeters inside to see who is at the door. The interior walls are six-inch-wide cedar boards with a saw-textured finish. The flooring is tongue-and-groove red oak, and the cabinetry is red oak veneer. The cabinets serve all the storage needs for the space. The continuous line

of cabinetry begins in the kitchen, stores china and flatware near the dining table, houses stereo components near the center, and serves as living-area storage adjacent to the fireplace. The countertop allows space for a buffet or food preparation.

Teel opted for structural trusses of four-by-six Douglas fir, rather than the more common Glulam beams—large beams made of laminated wood that have sufficient strength to support a roof with a single member and without a truss system. "I like trusses," he says. "They are more barnlike. More vernacular." The painting on the rear wall in egg tempera on paper is by Dickson Schneider and titled *Fish Table*. The sofa and chairs in the living area are from the Simona series by the Italian manufacturer Brunati. The coffee and dining tables are custom designs by Teel. The dining chairs are reproductions of Marcel Breuer's Cesca chair. The pendant light fixture above the breakfast bar is by Artemide. The track lighting, which runs at a cross-axis through the truss system, consists of a Lightolier track with Artemide Sintesi fixtures.

The overall effect of this living space is of a modernist rusticity punctuated with refined accoutrements—a basic house plan made grand through its details and careful choice of materials. Money saved through the modest square footage and simple plan is lavished on refined details and furniture. The Teel house is an excellent application of the loft living plan. The Teels have no children and use the house primarily as a private weekend retreat. In small, intimate households like this one, the loft plan functions extremely well.

The juxtaposition of the main bedroom and the living room can be seen from the exterior of the house at night.

The bedroom, on the ground floor, has a slate floor placed at grade. The ceiling is relatively low, but is made interesting with exposed Douglas fir beams. Noguchi lamps flank the bed. Two red leather chairs by Montis and an Artemide Aggregato floor lamp form a seating group in one corner.

Off the bedroom is a solarium, which doubles as a guest bedroom and reading room. With its floor on the same plane as the ground outside and its windows running floor to ceiling, the room extends visually and psychologically into the natural environment. This is Brenda Teel's favorite place to read, particularly during the winter rains. The windows have Castec Roman shades of white cotton duck. This simple and highly functional window treatment is used throughout the house.

The Teel house is a fine example of a functional, modernist approach softened by rustic and vernacular elements. Teel's philosophy was to build simply and straightforwardly and to allow the construction to be revealed. Floor and roof structural elements are exposed. The flooring on the first level is stone flooring; the second level is wood. The walls are clad in wood inside and out. Although the house has many refinements, a purposeful simplicity prevails—the Artemide fixtures use incandescent bulbs available at the local supermarket, the many solar features of the house are passive and do not require mechanical systems, the fireplace is the single source of heat upstairs, and the roof plan is a simple shed sloping toward the ocean.

TEEL HOUSE
OWNERS *Jeffrey and Brenda Teel*
ARCHITECT *Jefferey Teel*
DATE *Completed in 1986*
CONTRACTOR *Ralph Jackson*

## TOM AND KARIN'S PLACE

Set among a canopy of large trees is the second home of Tom Haines and Karin Swanson, which their architect, Obie Bowman, referred to as Tom and Karin's Place throughout design and construction. The name stuck. Karin Swanson and a friend impulsively purchased the lot in the early 1970s during a weekend drive up the coast. Prices then were not as high as they are now, and many early Sea Ranchers acquired their property in such acts of caprice. Karin Swanson eventually bought out her friend's interest so that she and her husband, Tom, could develop the land.

The house is a vertical, shingle-covered core with a simple peaked roof to which four appendages cling. The fireplace and entry sheds have cedar roofs that contrast dramatically with the black composition shingles of the core. A county building ordinance forbids wood roofs in the immediate presence of trees as a fire-retardant measure. However, Bowman noticed in the code that any surface with a slope in excess of sixty degrees is defined as a wall rather than a roof. This prompted him to design steep shed roofs for the appendages, which enforce the verticality of the core. The black shingles tend to silhouette the house, and the generous windows give it a transparency that enhances the sense of living in the woods and also reveals the narrowness of the building even when it is viewed from its long elevation.

Steps at the back of the house lead down to a hot tub set cozily beneath a giant redwood.

The massive redwood brackets on the retaining wall support a bench seat for the deck above.

The glass roof of the solarium brings the arching canopy of redwoods and Bishop pines into the house.

The communal areas are laid out in a loft plan with generous windows on the long sides. The living area, kitchen, and adjacent dining area in the solarium share the first floor. Above the kitchen is the cantilevered loft, which Haines and Swanson call a "nest." This retreat for reading or relaxing is lit by a skylight. The floors are vertical-grain fir.

A portal looks from the stairs into the loft, which can be closed off with a curtain like those used in hospitals. The structural framing of the stairwell is left exposed rather than covered. A pattern of cross-braces doubles as shelving for books and collectibles, a design Bowman has used in several of his houses. The floors of the loft are carpeted, and overscaled pillows invite lounging—an approach that adds to the nestlike quality of the space. The loft railing, the stair railing, and the railings leading to the hot tub were fabricated by Tom Haines and his son John.

The living room can be viewed from the loft. The large painting is by Haines's son John. Swanson's daughter Lisa DeLong, an interior designer, assisted with many of the design decisions in the living room and throughout the house. Haines's son John and Swanson's son Jim DeLong helped with all the tile work in the house, both in the bathrooms and on the patio. Haines's daughter Nancy also assisted with some projects. Haines and Swanson are very proud of the family effort that went into the house.

Wall shelves at the base of the stairs hold mid-nineteenth century woodworking tools, family heirlooms that Haines inherited from his great-grandfather. They interest him as sculptural objects and reflect his interest in woodworking.

Tom and Karin's Place exemplifies the compelling quality of a woods setting at Sea Ranch. Both the setting and the architectural solutions are a striking contrast to the meadows and the meadow houses. The house introduces new materials in the form of composition shingles for exterior walls, yet maintains the Sea Ranch tradition of wood roofs. The recent vintage of the house offers further evidence that the Sea Ranch approach to building and design can accommodate new concepts.

TOM AND KARIN'S PLACE
**OWNERS** *Tom Haines and Karin Swanson*
**ARCHITECT** *Obie Bowman*
**DATE** *Completed in 1994*
**CONTRACTOR** *Brian Dixon*

The Sea Ranch home of San Franciscans Ed and Kathleen Anderson emerges from a thicket of cypress trees at the ocean bluff above Walk On Beach. Completed in early 1990, it is one of many Sea Ranch commissions by San Francisco architect William Turnbull. Ed Anderson considers the grocery at Ocean Cove, a few miles south of Sea Ranch, as an important influence for the aesthetics of the house. Turnbull likens the Anderson house to a "taut" fisherman's cottage—charming, but tough. It is sided with cedar shingles and has wood-frame windows, a departure for Sea Ranch where black anodized aluminum is the norm. Turnbull describes the latter as "inexpensive and pragmatic" but feels that using wood exclusively is more in keeping with the Sea Ranch ideal.

Turnbull used slight changes in floor level to define the open spaces of the interior. The living area is set two steps below the dining area. The walls and floor are of vertical-grain fir, and the ceiling is horizontal-grain fir. The dining furniture is manufactured in Maine by Thos. Moser. The dark wood is cherry; the lighter is ash. The windows have snap-on canvas shades that the Andersons attach when they are away. Only the bedrooms have window coverings. The long corner window seat was Ed Anderson's idea for optimizing the sunlight while one enjoys the view or reads. Turnbull attributes the distinctive ceiling trusses to the influence of Finnish architect Alvar Aalto.

The rear hall makes a dogleg as it climbs to the master bedroom at the back of the house. The raised master bedroom affords a view of the coastline and ocean to the south. A casement window in the hall opens over a small hedge in the garden.

The kitchen, adjacent to the dining area, has cabinets of vertical-grain fir with Corian countertops. Glass in the front and back of the wall cabinets opens the kitchen to the hall beyond.

French doors behind the dining area open to a deck facing the ocean. Two Adirondack chairs provide comfortable seating for taking in the broad ocean view.

The lighting throughout the house consists of bare reflector bulbs that bounce light off the ceilings. This technique was first used at Sea Ranch in a house designed collaboratively by William Turnbull, Charles Moore, and Richard Peters. It is a simple, low-tech solution that produces a pleasing warm glow.

The guest bedroom faces the ocean and opens to the deck on the front of the house. The pencil-post bed, side table, and chest were handmade in North Carolina. The watercolor on the chest was a wedding present from San Francisco artist Christine M. High. The large painting of a nautical scene above the bed, as well as the smaller painting of a house on a knoll, came from an auction.

Both the kitchen and the dining area have French doors that open to the rear patio. The dining area, which features French doors forward and aft, can become almost an outdoor room. For the Andersons, dining on the patio overlooking the south-facing garden with their young daughters is a popular Sea Ranch experience. Turnbull emphasizes the importance of the nominally insular house, which can be opened grandly to the outdoors when the weather permits, as intrinsic to residential design in the Bay Area. He cites Charles Keeler's apt statement that "Hillside architecture is landscape gardening around a few rooms for use in case of rain." It eloquently characterizes the philosophy of the Anderson house.

A fence at the rear of the property encloses a formally landscaped yard. It is patterned directly after the fences of hand-hewn timbers that remain at Sea Ranch from the era when the property was a sheep ranch. The fence is an appropriate companion for the surrounding cypress trees and the rustic cedar shingles that clad the house.

Wood is vital to the ambience of this house. The roof, exterior walls, and windows and the interior walls, cabinets, ceilings, and floors are all wood. Even the pavers in the patio are wood.

ANDERSON HOUSE
**OWNERS**   *Ed and Kathleen Anderson*
**ARCHITECT**   *William Turnbull,*
*William Turnbull Associates*
**DATE**   *Completed in 1990*
**CONTRACTOR**   *Matt Sylvia,*
*Matthew Sylvia Construction Co.*

## TWILIGHT AT SEA RANCH

The day ends with a typically dramatic burst of color. As the sea, hills, and forests are bathed in amber, children enjoy the remainder of the day at Black Point Beach. A little farther north,

the sun sets into a fog bank hovering over the Pacific, silhouetting a barn house by Turnbull and Moore.

# Houses, Homes, and
## D R E A M S

WILLIAM TURNBULL, JR.

Houses come in many sizes and homes come in a diversity of styles. Making one is not necessarily synonymous with making the other. As an architect, I am fascinated with trying to make both at the same time. The secret is one of inhabitation, understanding the idiosyncrasies of the people we build for and, equally important, the unique qualities of the land they desire to build upon. Both are sources of inspiration and both will talk with you. The critical component is the ability to listen. Each will impart statistical information: "three bedrooms, two baths" or "a fifteen percent ground slope with prevailing westerly winds." But this is only a synopsis. One needs to hear the casual pieces of information, the asides and judgmental references, to understand fully the nature of the problem and the opportunity at hand. Design, in this regard, is like a detective story filled with clues that, it is hoped, lead to a skillful conclusion.

House design must have a story behind it to be coherent, an organization, an idea, for making the decisions comprehensible as a whole. Buildings also have an order, but it is a hierarchy of organization: rooms, corridors, and closets or the construction techniques themselves. Instead of words the designer works with spaces, the voids, the "empties" that are enclosed by walls. It is those spaces, perceived in light, that are the building blocks. This differs from the sculptor, who works with solid objects and masses, and the painter, who deals with surfaces upon which to put color. The architect's vocabulary is space. Like a book, to be successful, a house should also have an idea. Without some spatially organizing concept, rooms rattle around each other, butt into halls, and are strung together like a pearl necklace. Such a result might be a beautiful adornment, but may be difficult to inhabit.

That brings up the second critical element of good house design: livability. In the 1970s, Chris Alexander compiled a huge encyclopedic tome called *A Pattern Language,* describing how people lived in various spaces and situations. Living is not all that complicated, and essentially a matter of common sense. Spaces determine their uses, and if you pause long enough to look at the swirl of life eddying around you, it will become clear that people need different kinds of spaces for sleeping, for cooking, for eating, and for socializing, not to mention areas for personal ablutions. When I work on a house design, the floor plan always includes some furniture doodles. Not that this is the way someone might actually furnish his or her room, but to satisfy myself that the heirloom four-poster or treasured futon actually will fit comfortably in the spaces I design.

The first house at the Sea Ranch, for a young lawyer friend, was only 564 square feet. It was a little house, but simultaneously it wanted to be a grand house commanding a twenty-mile view of magnificent California coastline. We made the center octagonal, holding up a sheltering pyramidal roof. The posts for the octagonal frame were inexpensive round cores from the plywood mills, the leftovers after flitches for plywood had been skinned away. As we needed more space beyond this fourteen-foot center, we extended the roof: for a double-bed space facing the water, a closet and a compartmented bathroom under the hip, a tiny (too tiny) dining space under another hip, a step-up entry/mud room with wall pegs in lieu of a closet, a miniature L-shaped kitchen, and finally a place for the record player and records. All this in 564 square feet. The inhabitation requirements spatially shaped the house spiraling out from the central order of the formal octagon.

No house, however, is a complete entity without its integration to the site it inhabits. Perhaps this is why trailer houses look so forlorn in their shining armor, crouching on their allotted pieces of ground. Donlyn Lyndon has allowed that buildings can either mark or merge, enclose or enfront their surroundings. Essentially this is correct, but it is the permutations and combinations of these ideas that lead to memorable situations.

THE SEA RANCH SITE
*Courtesy William Turnbull Associates*

The first condominium at the Sea Ranch was a demonstration example of clustered housing for the developer: proof that congregate housing could enhance rather than destroy the vulnerable short-grass landscape at the rocky edge of the continent. To this end we amassed a complex of ten units grouped around two courtyards: one for the wind protection of its inhabitants and the other to corral and contain the shiny automotive products of Detroit and Japanese technology. The site, approached by Highway 1 from the south, is visible from more than three miles away. The roofline of the units slopes upward to follow the landform (merging) and is topped at the rocky crag with the three-story tower of Unit 10 (a marker). Here, in one composition, on the tough salt-swept edge of the sea, we employed three of the devices in one composition. Unsoftened by foundation or other plantings (nothing likes to grow in this harsh environment), the condominium is a wooden rock, its weathered redwood walls matching the color of its geologic cousins and marking a place of shelter, community, and inhabitation.

A house, to be memorable and special, needs to interweave these components: a specific landscape, the invitation for inhabitation, and an encompassing idea or metaphor that serves as an umbrella to shelter the specifics of a detailed design.

But the designer or architect cannot get much further than this. A house, a shelter, physically and intellectually, does not engender the poignancy of the word *home*. Home is the idiosyncrasy of inhabitation which can range from collections of family memorabilia to exotic manifestations of an individual personality: Sir John Soane to Charles Moore or an Irish Fisherman's cottage to a Hollywood Hacienda. The inescapable measurement of home is you; who you are or what you are as measured by the looking glass of the spaces you live in.

Here the reality of design as a mutual adventure comes into play. A designer/architect can help you sort out your priorities, but can never be a satisfactory surrogate inhabitant without you. Your likes and dislikes, the innuendo of life, your perceptions of the appropriate, all play in the equation as you try to build, or rebuild, a place to live in that gives you both pleasure and delight.

What is occurring here is the pursuit of dreams: one's own special place on the planet, the dream house of Mr. Blandings in the 1948 movie, or the English castle of Mr. Shakespeare. Dream houses are the property of us all: young of age and heart, or old and gray with thinning hair. The other characteristic of dreams is usually a paucity of funds to achieve our images, be they memories of other times and places, or clippings garnered and carefully kept from the glossy colored pages of the shelter magazines. But budgets need not be an enemy. They can assist in honing our desires and clarifying what is truly important for each of us. This is a personal game of monopoly where hot-tub dollars are traded for a working fireplace, and the square footage we actually need to live well is balanced against symbolic street facades.

But for our dreams of houses or dream houses to exist at all, there needs to be a piece of ground to rest upon, to become reality. This is a far deeper dream that predates our historic memory. Land ownership and the congruency of personal freedom fueled our original colonies and the gigantic fire of westward expansion, eventually leading to the golden land of California and the Pacific Coast. From Daniel Boone to the dust bowl immigrants, land was an irresistibly powerful magnet, and it was not until the middle of this present century that the Homestead Act was officially abolished. Now land is becoming an even dearer commodity. As the population swells to turn a new century, it will become even more so. The utopian plans for Broadacre City or various Levittown models of suburbia have given way to town-house condominiums with code-prescribed minimal rear-yard allotments of open space. Within this shrinking resource, dreamers must find their rainbow's end. Unlike previous generations, they will not have boundless horizons or unlimited space, but will have to make do with neighbors whose proximity will vary with their economic means. This reality, like that of limited construction budgets, should not be a source of despair, but a discipline of clearer values.

What is done with the land is as important as what is done with the dream house itself, especially and most dramatically in the benevolent and temperate microclimates some of us live in across the United States. As there are dreams for houses, there are also dreams for gardens, the outdoor rooms of our habitation. Charles Keeler, a Californian, just after the turn of the century, defined architecture in the Bay Area as garden rooms with occasional roofs in case of rain. The horticultural manipulation of our surroundings can establish privacy, where that is important, or intellectually transport us through collections of exotics to distant places. Simple masses of colorful plantings can just brighten our day or, as in the case of snowdrops, remind us of the end of a dismally long, gray winter.

This personalization of land transforms a landscape the same way home transforms a house. In designing one, the other should be considered with equal energy, care, and affection.

Architecture, and by that I only mean thoughtful building, has been described as one generation's gift to the next. That definition can be broadened to include landscape architecture or, less pretentiously, gardening. What we do as makers of these places reveals our passions and prejudices as clearly as footprints in mud, dust, or sand. The clarity and order of our thoughts give back great pleasure to ourselves or, as storytellers, to the audience of our visitors. For hearth and home are the mythic base of our civilization, and each of us, in our generation, invariably interprets these in our own way. For the architect/designer, it is a privilege to go along on the journey as a conceptual midwife. For our role, at least for houses, has always been that of a dream maker.

section **2**

THE NEW TOWN   THE OLD WAYS

# Seaside

SEASIDE PORCHES

Visitors to Seaside socialize on the

porch of one of the Honeymoon

Cottages. The revival of southern

porch culture is one of the

community's primary goals.

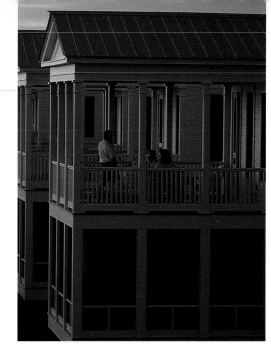

**SEASIDE** is a new town begun in the early 1980s set on eighty acres of land that fronts the Gulf of Mexico in the Florida panhandle. It is reached by County Road 30-A, a short loop to the coast off Highway 98. The location of Seaside, relative to large metropolitan areas, is fairly remote. The closest urban area with a population of over a million is New Orleans, which is about two hundred sixty miles to the west. Birmingham, its metropolitan area possessing a population just under a million, is about an equal distance away. Atlanta, the largest city within a reasonable driving distance, is about three hundred miles away. Miami, and the substantial population of south Florida, is a considerable driving distance away from the panhandle, over six hundred miles.

## SEAGROVE BEACH HOUSES

The houses at Seagrove Beach, Seaside's

neighbor to the east, were built after

World War II and set in thick groves of

scrub oaks, magnolias, and gnarly sand

pines. Modest single-story beach cabins,

usually incorporating screened porches, are

the predominant type.

Abutting Seaside to the east is Seagrove Beach, a typically platted beach development established after World War II. It is distinctive for being set in a thick grove of scrub oaks and magnolias. To the west is a narrow finger of undeveloped land owned by St. Joe Paper Co., a large landholder in the area. St. Joe clear-cut the forests to the west and north of Seaside and lets these lands lie fallow. These areas await development of some sort, as they are too sandy for agricultural use. Farther west is Grayton State Park, a coastal park that surrounds the town of Grayton Beach, Seaside's closest neighbor to the west, only a couple of miles away. Grayton is the oldest beach town in this part of the panhandle. Many of its

buildings are clapboard cabins built between the world wars. The town's architecture is richly weathered, and its streets are partially submerged by sand encroaching from the dunes at Grayton State Park. Its ambience is laid-back. I like to think of Grayton as being much like Key West in Ernest Hemingway's time.

The broader context of the Florida coast from Ft. Walton Beach on the west to Panama City on the east can be characterized as surreal kitsch. Had not the Las Vegas strip been the inspiration for Venturi, Scott Brown, and Izenour's 1972 book, *Learning From Las Vegas*, this beach strip known colloquially as the

"Redneck Riviera" would have done just fine. It is a linear strip development of curious roadside attractions, cinder-block motels, and shopping centers, with an occasional condo tower of ten or more stories. Here one can bungee jump, play "Goofy Golf," purchase a beach towel emblazoned with the Confederate flag, or partake of Jello shooters at a boisterous roadside joint. This area is historically the recreational turf of southwest Georgia, south Alabama, and the inland areas of the panhandle. Since the 1970s it has had a much broader following, attracting people from outside the region. It remains, however, hardly a location where one would expect to find an innovative community like Seaside.

Seaside was developed by Robert Davis, who had never taken on a development of this scale, though he had some successful and award-winning developments to his credit. Nor did he have any previous experience in developments that included anything other than residential units. He hired Andres Duany and Elizabeth Plater-Zyberk, a husband-and-wife planning team then at the Miami firm of Arquitectonica, to plan the development. Duany and Plater-Zyberk were recent Yale University graduates with no substantial national reputation when they were asked to design Seaside. Their mentor was Leon Krier, an architecture/planning theorist born in Luxembourg, who in the early 1980s was living in London. At the time Seaside was begun, Krier had never had any of his designs built, though he had gained an international reputation as a polemicist who reveled in controversy. It may seem improbable that these individuals would converge on eighty acres in the

SHACK O' THE HILLS

GRAYTON BEACH HOUSE

Grayton Beach, just to the west of Seaside, is the setting for this single-story, frame cottage resting on cinder-block piers. Most likely built between the world wars, it is a fine example of a vernacular beach cabin and is a key prototype for early Seaside cottages. The screened porch fronting the street and the narrow form—at most two rooms wide—allow good cross-ventilation. The cottage has weathered attractively in the coastal climate. After this photograph was taken, the cottage was refreshed with new paint and a new roof, but soon it will look like this again.

middle of the Redneck Riviera to create a town which the January 1990 issue of *Time* featured as one of the most significant design achievements of the 1980s and described as "the most astounding design achievement of its era and, one might hope, the most influential."

The eighty acres comprising Seaside were purchased in 1946 by Robert Davis's grandfather, Joseph Smolian, who intended to develop the property as a holiday camp for the employees of the Birmingham department store Pizitz, in which he was a partner. The model was Camp Helen, located about ten miles east at Phillip's Inlet, which was the employee camp for Avondale Mills. However, Smolian's business partner, Isidore Pizitz, nixed the idea as a needless waste of money. Smolian held on to his deed, confident that the value of the land would appreciate over time.

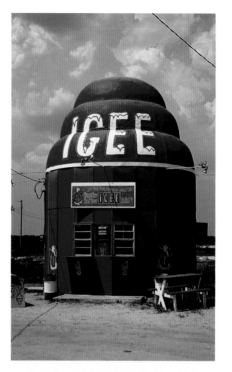

From time to time, ideas for developing the land would surface. In the late 1960s, when Robert Davis had just graduated from Antioch College, Smolian hired a real estate consultant practicing in the panhandle to plat a conventional development. They got as far as cutting some roads through the scrubby landscape when the plan was

dropped. The name for this never-built development was Dreamland Heights, the name later given to Seaside's first downtown building designed by New York architect Steven Holl.

In the mid-1970s Smolian bequeathed a few acres from his parcel to the University of Alabama, a school he had supported in numerous ways over the years. By this time Robert Davis had developed a strong interest in real estate development and became involved in planning a use for this parcel for the university. The initial idea was to create a conference center, but the university failed to seize the initiative and follow through. By the late 1970s, the university seemed ready to proceed. Davis became reinvolved and went so far as to engage Arquitectonica to explore designs for a conference center or an academic retreat. Susan Lewin, then an editor at *House Beautiful*, had recommended that Davis discuss his project with the firm. Arquitectonica had just received a *Progressive Architecture* award for a Miami apartment building that first brought some national recognition to the firm. Early in his discussions with Arquitectonica, Davis gravitated

REDNECK RIVIERA

Roadside beach stores, beach cabins, and

attractions such as "Goofy Golf" were

among the first wave of development on

the Gulf Coast of Florida's panhandle.

The strongly regional patronage of the

area earned it the nickname Redneck

Riviera. This concatenation of largely

unmanaged development forms the broad

context for Seaside.

toward two of its principals, Andres Duany and Elizabeth Plater-Zyberk. However, their plans for an academic retreat, which included simple cabins on a curving street tangential to the Gulf, were ultimately rejected by the university. The entire project seemed too speculative and outside the university's purpose and budget. Within a few years, Davis realized that the university would never do anything with the land, and he repurchased it so it could be developed in accordance with the grand scheme that was beginning to take shape.

As Duany and Plater-Zyberk, or DPZ as their post-Arquitectonica design practice is known, began planning what ultimately became Seaside, they were influenced by a concurrent commission, Charleston Place, in Boca Raton, Florida. Charleston Place was their first built community that attempted to create an urbanity that automobile suburbs lacked. Since moving to south Florida, a pervasively suburban landscape, they recognized the absence of any meaningful urban environment. They wanted to incorporate in Charleston Place mixed-use buildings and small street setbacks to give the development a more urban feeling. To their surprise, they discovered that many of the elements they wanted to include— elements intrinsic to older towns and cities—were illegal under the current codes.

Through subterfuge, DPZ attempted to get approval for their plan. For instance, they learned that very few rules applied to parking lots. So in the plans for Charleston Place they labeled the streets "parking lots" in order to get approval for a smaller setback. The codes they worked under specified large minimal

setbacks from house to street, but parking lots were not similarly controlled. A house could be adjacent to a parking lot, but not to a street. The planning goal of such thinking is to facilitate maximum vehicular speed on the street. If houses are too close to the street, motorists will feel compelled to slow down and will impair the traffic flow. Accommodating the automobile drives the entire process.

For Seaside, as for Charleston Place, Duany and Plater-Zyberk were commissioned to plan the community and design the houses within it. However, they had learned something from Charleston Place: because DPZ had designed all of the houses, the community lacked the interesting architectural variety of a town whose buildings are designed by many different architects over a span of time. Early in their work on Seaside, they decided that they would develop a master plan, but would not design any of its buildings. Another reason for this decision was that Robert Davis had well-defined expectations for the houses of Seaside. He did not want postmodern

houses—contemporary interpretations of historical architecture—but instead wanted vernacular architecture in the tradition of the region. This type of architecture, DPZ felt, called for a more grass roots approach—where sensitive builders and laypeople, complemented by an occasional commission by an independent architect, would produce the most appropriate architecture. This, after all, is the tradition of vernacular architecture.

Once Duany and Plater-Zyberk had defined their role as planners writing a code, rather than architects designing buildings, the concept of Seaside as more than a development began to emerge. What Davis wanted as a developer, and what they were prepared to deliver as planners, were the ingredients for a new town.

In 1980 Davis and his wife moved into a rented house in the neighboring town of Grayton Beach. As Duany and Plater-Zyberk refined their town plan, the Davises began to mobilize for its construction. A simple wood deck with a small pavilion overlooking the Gulf, at the center of Seaside's beach frontage was built in 1981, followed by a small red house with a cupola atop a pyramidal hip roof. This house, designed by Davis, became the first Seaside sales office. Next to it Davis built another house of his own design as the Davises' residence. The yellow, single-story clapboard house in a southern vernacular was completed in 1982. Robert and Daryl Davis were the first residents of Seaside and continue to live there full-time. Having outgrown the yellow house, they are in their second house, which is on Seaside Avenue.

In 1982, Davis's grandfather, Joseph Smolian, died. He had lived to see the plan for Seaside and the completion of these first modest structures, but remained uncertain that this development was a good idea. On Smolian's death, Davis inherited the parcel that would become Seaside.

With a town plan by Duany and Plater-Zyberk, the Davis's hands-on oversight, and grand promises of what Seaside would become, lots sold briskly. Early on, Seaside clearly gained acceptance from a public expressing a voracious demand for this kind of development. What made Duany and Plater-Zyberk's town plan so compelling and Seaside such a spectacular success?

Duany and Plater-Zyberk believed that towns should be designed around people. Accompanied by Robert and Daryl Davis and on their own, they explored small-town America at length, trying to get at the heart of what made it successful. They observed the widths of streets, the distance from streets to houses, the layout of street grids—anything that might explain why the house, the street, the square, the town was successful. Observations of the traditional small town taken from this informal field research drove the process of designing Seaside. DPZ is a strong advocate of observing local architectural types to determine appropriate design responses. Duany contends that this approach is much faster than studying and analyzing charts of local climate, wind patterns, topography, and the like. Trust that your predecessors figured these elements out a long time ago. By analyzing their solutions and selectively incorporating them, an appropriate architectural design will follow.

Relative to automobile suburbia, Seaside is best characterized as incorporating much of what is popular with suburbia—detached, single-family houses as the most common residential type and the absence of high-rise density. But, unlike suburbia, Seaside incorporates much of what is desirable about the city—convenient services, compelling public places, and the potential for varied and stimulating social interaction. The core principle of Seaside is to be a town where homes, services, shops, and recreation can be reached by walking rather than driving. For the walk to be brief, about five minutes from periphery to center, buildings must be relatively close together. Lots need to be small and setbacks minimal for a walking city to work. Aesthetic issues are at play as well. Houses with a minimal setback form an urban, architectural streetscape, in contrast to the more substantial setbacks in automobile suburbs, where street vistas are formed by lawns, planted trees, and driveways. At the core of Seaside is its downtown: a village green incorporating an amphitheater surrounded by mixed-use commercial buildings.

Walking needed to be convenient, but it also needed to be stimulating and enjoyable. Much of the planning effort at Seaside centered on providing street vistas that terminate at points of geographic or architectural interest. Interconnected streets and paths offer many varying, but uniformly convenient, routes to reach various points within the community.

Robert Davis notes frequently in his talks on community planning issues that something is amiss in a society where individuals drive to an exercise club to then jump on a treadmill to get the exercise they would have had if only they had meaningful places to walk. At Seaside, the need for treadmills has been supplanted with a way of life where walking is convenient and stimulating.

The plan of Seaside begins as a traditional town, but from there it gets more complex. Architectural historian Dennis Doordan, who was a scholar-in-residence at Seaside in January 1995, made an insightful observation on his experience there. "My expectation was that Seaside would be a small southern town. Instead, I found it to be a hybrid community—more urban, more complex, with more architectural diversity and higher density than a small town would ever have. Also, conspicuous things that all southern towns have, like a Baptist church, are missing." Though DPZ drew from the tradition of the small southern town, they did not re-create one. Those in the media who have interpreted Seaside as a nostalgic repackaging of small-town America either have failed to grasp the depth of its urbanity or have oversimplified it.

The traditional urbanism of Seaside, where home, work, and shopping are integrated in a single community, is a striking contrast to the development pattern typically found in edge cities. Andres Duany put it succinctly when he noted in a Toronto lecture in 1991 that each year in Florida alone the equivalent of twelve new towns are created, but these

TYPE

DESCRIPTION:

LOCATION:
INTENDED USE

PROTOTYPE:

TYPE

DESCRIPTION:

LOCATION:
INTENDED USE

PROTOTYPE:

TYPE

DESCRIPTION:

LOCATION:
INTENDED USE

PROTOTYPE:

TYPE

DESCRIPTION:
LOCATION:
INTENDED USE

PROTOTYPE:

on the prescriptions in the Seaside Urban Code, a document whose purpose is to establish a coherent building pattern of integrated use, rather than to mandate segregated uses, as the unifunctional zoning of suburbia typically does. A further purpose of the code is to ensure that the details of a given building type are appropriate and compatible with neighboring houses. It is not, however, intended to mandate style. Aesthetic and planning issues are continually confused, and this confusion has certainly been inflicted on Seaside. The architecture of Seaside is largely traditional, and the Construction Regulations, a document separate from the Urban Code, are the major determinant of that traditionalism through the mandating of such elements as operable wood windows, tin roofs, wood siding, and exposed rafter tails. Regional vernacular architecture was analyzed and then its intrinsic elements were specified in the regulations to achieve the architectural language desired by Robert Davis for Seaside's buildings.

PAVILIONS

All Seaside streets perpendicular to the

Gulf, such as Savannah and Odessa

streets shown here, terminate at a

pavilion through which Seasiders access

the beach.

The need for eight building types was not just to ensure architectural diversity, though this was an important role. The various types accommodate different intended uses and are ordered so that the density of the town gradually increases in proximity to the central square at the town center. Most of the types, except in special situations where the prescriptions are quite liberal, have a clearly identifiable, historical prototype. For example, the villas of Seaside Avenue (type IV) have as their prototype the antebellum mansions of the American South. The "Charleston" (type VII) is based on the side-yard single house of Charleston, South Carolina. The row houses of Ruskin Place (type III) have the Pontalba Buildings of Jackson Square in New Orleans as their prototype. The "bungalows" (type VI) of Seaside's north-south streets have a more widely varied, but nonetheless discernible prototype—the narrow, suburban or small-town bungalow, one story or one and a half stories, with a prominent front porch. This typically vernacular building is commonly embellished with restrained historical detailing, from Folk Victorian to Arts and Crafts.

As Duany and Plater-Zyberk were in the midst of planning Seaside, they sent a fairly developed draft of the town plan to their mentor Leon Krier for his review and suggestions. Krier's involvement led to several changes in the final plan for the town. One of the most significant was his proposal for including a network of easements through the town which formed public pathways called sandpaths. Like sidewalks, they can be used to get anywhere in the community, including the beach.

The sandpaths are defined by low wood picket fences required at the property lines of residential lots. These fences must be painted a uniform white, and no two fences on a given block can be exactly alike. All residential lots, but *not* the mixed-use lots in the town center and Ruskin Place, are configured to border both a vehicular street and a pedestrian sandpath.

The Seaside Urban Code is complemented by the Construction Regulations for houses. These two documents, working in concert, form the building controls for the town. All building requirements are plainly spelled out. For instance, in regard to roofing material, the regulations do not state, in the manner of Sea Ranch guidelines, that roofing materials must be of a type and material appropriate to vernacular buildings. Rather, the guidelines state that wood shake, metal shingle, corrugated metal sheet, V-crimp metal sheet, or standing seam metal sheet may be used. Simply pick from one of these or ask for a variance. The Construction Regulations are purposefully simple so that laypeople can readily understand them. The intent is that an architect should not be considered essential for the design of a Seaside house. A few other notable requirements in the regulations are that windows must be of wood and must be square or vertical in proportion, not horizontal. Roofs must be pitched, and the slopes of the pitch are specified. All plans are required to go through a design review process. The intent of the Construction Regulations is to ensure that Seaside houses have commonality of materials and roof type. It is a shared attitude toward these elements that, DPZ feels, makes for a coherent urbanity.

The Seaside streets with a north-south axis terminate at County Road 30-A. Across from each street terminus is a pavilion and dune walkover that provides access to the beach. The pavilions, in the tradition of grand architectural follies, are some of the community's most fanciful and whimsical architecture. More significantly, they are an integral civic asset used by all Seasiders. Even property owners who reside on the beach side of 30-A must use the pavilion walkovers to access the beach. No private walkovers are allowed. Therefore, the approximately one-half-mile beach frontage of Seaside is shared by all. Everyone uses the same access, follows the same rules, and stakes claims to beach turf on a first-come basis whether they live right on the Gulf or in the corner of town farthest from it. The beach, the most important amenity of the town, is a communal asset whose identity as such has been enforced through socially deterministic planning.

The houses of Seaside are oriented not to the Gulf but to their brick-paved streets. By embracing the street as a vital public place, they connect their occupants to the community. The broad street and town vistas in the pictorial section that follows were all taken from vantage points in private residences. A significant characteristic of every Seaside house is that the residents can visually experience the community around them. These beckoning vistas remind Seasiders that their community is embedded in a special natural environment.

The houses at Seaside are distinctive for their polychrome wood siding, metal roofs, and generous porches that are typically screened. No two houses on any given block can be painted the same color. With white originally reserved for public buildings, the variety of color in the house facades was considered important for fostering a varied streetscape. The metal roofs provide perhaps the strongest vernacular suggestion for the Seaside house. Metal roofs are typically found only on barns and other farm buildings within the region and are perceived as being cheap and utilitarian. Indeed, there has been some debate over the appropriateness of metal roofs in a climate with corrosive, salt-laden air. These roofs last about ten to twelve years and then have to be replaced. There are, however, two primary attributes that determine the appropriateness of a building material: durability and easy, cheap replacement. A material must meet one of the two to be practical. The metal roof is cheap and easy to replace provided that the roof plan is relatively simple. Some of Seaside's more recent houses do have quite complex roof plans, and ultimately this may present a maintenance problem for their owners.

The porch, though, is clearly the most important architectural attribute of the Seaside house. It is equally important to the neighborliness desired for the community. Porches are a key transitional space. They form an important link between the private realm of the home and the public realm of the street. The residents' frequent use of this vital transitional space gives the community a populated ambience. The bottom line is that Seasiders seem genuinely to enjoy the porch as a treasured attribute of their houses.

A tin roof, a porch, a polychrome paint scheme, and a white picket fence at the property line became defining elements of Seaside residential architecture. This combination of highly iconographic components is complemented by a surrounding landscape of indigenous palmettos, sand pines, and scrub oaks poking through an underlayment of pine straw. In the early days of Seaside, Douglas Duany, landscape architect and brother of Andres, championed the fragile, Gulf Coast landscape at Seaside. He helped protect the existing vegetation when the first streets were laid and worked with early builders to ensure that little of the natural environment was disturbed during construction. Ultimately, this oversight was manifested in the Construction Regulations, which stipulate that only the area beneath the footprint of the building may be cleared for construction. The remainder of the vegetation on the lot must be left undisturbed. Douglas Duany promoted the indigenous landscape in other ways. He first put forth the concept that the open space at Ruskin Place should consist of a lower plaza and an upper "sacred grove," a protected area of indigenous sand pines and palmettos. In recent years, however, much of Douglas Duany's early landscaping, which featured indigenous planting, has been radically relandscaped.

Seaside's indigenous landscape was initially intended to be a more significant element in the scheme of things. But as Douglas Duany commented, "As the architecture of Seaside was amped up, the indigenous landscape was amped down." There have been a few ill-advised and inappropriate landscaping programs, and perhaps because of past mistakes, there has been within the community an emphasis on promoting indigenous plantings and fostering an appreciation for the preexisting landscape.

An important specification within the Seaside Urban Code was the allowance for outbuildings on most lots. Interestingly, outbuildings are rarely allowed in automobile suburbia because they potentially breach the low-density program of one household per lot or may be the setting for an activity or hobby deemed inappropriate for the community. In Seaside, outbuildings are encouraged for the many positive things they offer. They provide varied architectural scale and are ideal as guest cottages and as studios. Initially, it was hoped that some of Seaside's outbuildings might even be offered as economical long-term rentals, a prospect that would have enhanced socioeconomic diversity by giving renters a place within the community. However, this potential remains unrealized due to the marketability of outbuildings for transient accommodations during the summer. As Robert Davis put it, "No one is going to rent out their one-bedroom cottage annually for $400 a month, when it will rent for $1,000 per week in the summer."

In primary-home communities, outbuildings increase socioeconomic diversity by mixing owners and renters together. They provide a setting for creative and professional endeavors in the neighborhood, giving it

SUBURBAN HOUSE AND GARDEN

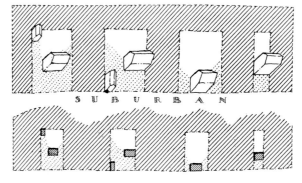

URBAN HOUSE AND GARDEN

—Courtesy Leon Krier

more life during the day, and they offer an important lifestyle option for those who like to work at home. They provide good settings for in-laws and extended-family living arrangements, and transitional accommodations for children preparing to leave the nest. Over the tenure of a household at a given address, the same outbuilding may serve all these purposes and then some. The outbuildings in Seaside may come to serve many of these same uses.

When Seaside was planned, the expectation was that the houses in the community would be designed in the vernacular language. This was the tradition of the immediate region. The Construction Regulations were specifically intended to suggest it. There was also an assumption that purchasers of Seaside lots would not

SUBURBAN AND URBAN STREETSCAPES

Leon Krier contrasts suburban and urban attitudes toward the formation of a streetscape. The scale, mass, and form of the architecture are similar, as are the lot sizes. Urbanity is a function of minimal setbacks and an intimate streetscape consistently formed by architecture. Suburbanity is a function of maximizing distances between buildings and of an incidental placement of architecture relative to the street.

The second wave of development through the Florida panhandle reflected the area's emerging status in the late 1960s as a resort of national significance. Cabins that were second homes for single families gave way to high-rise condominium towers and low-rise town-house condominiums. This pattern of development reached a frenzy in the late 1970s, just before the building of Seaside. Here, at Destin, about twenty miles west of Seaside, most of the concepts of Le Corbusier's *Ville Radieuse* are attempted: Residential towers dotting the landscape are separated by open space. Relatively high density is maintained while much space is left open. Wide thoroughfares, with few cross streets, accommodate the essential automobile.

have the construction or design budget to commission much beyond a vernacular building. This turned out not to be the case. The notion of "style" in the architecture of the private residences of Seaside was first introduced in Rosewalk, an early cluster of fourteen cottages designed by a single architectural firm headed by Robert Orr and Melanie Taylor. The small Rosewalk cottages were embellished with Folk Victorian elements—simple turrets, slant-sided window bays, decorative brackets, millwork on porches, scalloped shingles on gables, and so forth. The early and widely published Rosewalk contributed greatly to the popular notion of Seaside as a neo-Victorian village, which it isn't. Rosewalk, in fact, is unique within Seaside, but its introduction of architectural style to Seaside became indelible. Rosewalk was quickly followed by houses designed in styles with grander pretensions. John Massengale, during his tenure as Seaside's town architect in 1985 and 1986, designed the first Seaside house in the classical language, near the Savannah Pavilion. He admired the classical residential architecture of the antebellum South, felt it appropriate to the residences of Seaside, and facilitated his cause by granting himself a variance to the requirement on broad roof overhangs. Following the precedent that Massengale had established, the classical language was adopted for private residences, initially in a restrained manner, but eventually more grandly elaborated. Other styles became popular, and of the eclectic examples, most are fine houses. But the original vision of a town with simple, polychrome, vernacular frame cottages complemented by white classical public buildings can never be realized.

When considering the quantity and mandated diversity of architectural type within the community, it becomes apparent that the appropriation of languages

other than the vernacular was not arbitrary and capricious, but necessary. Some of Seaside's coded building types did not have strong associations with the vernacular. For instance, the antebellum mansion (type IV) and the Charleston single house (type VII) are associated with the classical tradition. The vernacular quite possibly could have been the dominant impression—I think it probably is—but it would have been overburdened as the only residential architectural language in Seaside. Seaside's architects sensed this and responded accordingly, and so did the code. The debate centers only on whether

or not the use of style as a vehicle to achieve architectural variety was overdone.

It is important to the Seaside ideal that construction materials be honest. Wood siding, for instance, needs to be genuine. Aluminum siding and laminated sheet goods designed to look like wood siding are not allowed. Wood cups, assumes a gnarly, pronounced grain, must be repainted frequently, and rots quite

readily in the coastal climate of Seaside. Maintenance would be required, and this was considered acceptable. Historically, architecture has always required maintenance, and Davis and DPZ concluded that if the Seaside community was going to have good architecture, built of the most appropriate materials, maintenance would have to be accepted.

The great achievement for Seaside, from the standpoint of real estate development, is that lots throughout the town were sold for prices comparable to the value of land on the Gulf. The conventional wisdom had been that everybody wants to be on the Gulf for the convenience, the views, and the guaranteed beach access. This thinking resulted in exorbitant land prices on the Gulf and a sharp falloff for land on the "wrong" side of the beach road. This situation drove high-rise development on the fragile, ecologically sensitive dunes, as high-rises provided maximum capitalization for the most valuable real estate.

In the case of Seaside, effective planning made property on the wrong side of the beach road just as desirable, and hence as valuable, as that on the Gulf. The short walk by street or sandpath to the beach is enjoyable and stimulating. The pavilions grandly symbolize egalitarian access to the beach. The significant infrastructure of sandpaths, streets, and pavilions allayed any fear that a lot in Seaside might not be as enjoyable and convenient as one on the Gulf.

From a marketing standpoint, Seaside was innovative in another way. As Andres Duany noted in an

An oblique aerial view taken in the winter of

1994 shows the entire town of Seaside.

The residential areas of the community are

largely complete. The downtown, to consist

of mixed-use buildings of three to five

stories, remains incomplete. The entire site

is only eighty acres, yet will ultimately

contain just over three hundred individual

homesites, many with outbuildings, as

many as two hundred hotel rooms and

apartments, about thirty mixed-use

rowhouses, and fifty thousand square feet

of commercial space with enough retail to

serve adjoining communities as well as

Seaside. The homes, services, and beach

can be reached by a walk of less than ten

minutes duration.

*—Courtesy Alex Maclean © 1994*

interview, in contemporary times two factors have increased the value of property. The first is quantity: a house is worth more if it has a large amount of land around it. More land equals more privacy and more prestige, and offers possibilities for land-intensive amenities like private swimming pools. The other factor is view: a house or an apartment with a view is worth more than an identical residence without one. A generous portion of land and a worthwhile view are two amenities that contemporary society has proven it will pay for. Seaside, Duany notes, revived a long-neglected third factor in the equation of real estate values: community. A lot in Seaside, because it is in a community with services, shops, and amenities that are convenient and close by, and because it is designed to be neighborly, is worth more than a lot in a neighborhood without these characteristics.

Evaluated solely from the marketing standpoint of successfully having *sold* the concept of community,

Seaside can be categorized as nothing less than a complete success. But the more significant question is whether socially deterministic planning *created* community. Although it is still too early to draw final conclusions, my observation is that community has definitely been created, a much better community than typically found in automobile suburbia.

Community at Seaside has taken time to evolve, as would certainly be the case for any new development. Not everyone who bought into the concept in its early days realized what the commitments truly entailed. They understood the part about traditional architecture, but they didn't necessarily understand the part about Seaside being a community with attributes altogether different from those of automobile suburbia. The town, designed to promote community and be more convenient for everybody, was not there yet. Only a few houses had been built. It was not clear or easy to communicate in the abstract the attributes of the ultimate Seaside experience. The town was only a developer's promise. Most early Seasiders hoped the town would be realized, but did not perceive it to be a mandatory part of the deal. Seaside now has an elected Town Council and a paid Town Manager. Most of their key, early issues have addressed such mundane concerns as garbage collection, parking control, and security. However, the council members' concern for keeping the streets pedestrian-friendly and more efficient for the walker than the driver is an important sign that they understand that their town has priorities different from those of automobile suburbia.

As important as the Town Council to the nurturing of community is the Seaside Institute. A nonprofit organization run and largely funded by community volunteers, it sponsors an ambitious schedule of events, lectures, festivals, and exhibits that enrich life in the town and draw people into the public forum. "Escape To Create," an artist/scholar-in-residence program whose participants are required to perform community service during their residencies in Seaside, is sponsored during the winter months. The Seaside Prize is awarded annually to chosen individuals who have made a major achievement toward the creation or visualization of better communities. In the winter of 1994, the Seaside Institute received its first major grant from the Florida Humanities Council, for a project titled "Making Florida Home: Lessons from Seaside." This is a community that wants to have influence, and it is making a formalized effort to achieve its goal.

Vincent Scully commented during his speech given on accepting the Seaside Prize in 1993 that Seaside had been a pleasant revelation to him. His former students, Duany and Plater-Zyberk, had resurrected what he had given up for lost: the traditional, pedestrian-oriented town plan. There is a modality of thinking that architecture has only two relevant "periods": archaic and postarchaic. What is now considered archaic has invariably been superceded by something more available, more cost-effective, more efficient. Just about everyone, including even Scully, was ready to concede that traditional urbanism and the walking city were things of the past, a treasured way of life fondly remembered but hopelessly archaic. The presence of Seaside proves otherwise. Through a carefully conceived Urban Code, supplemented by an equally considered set of Construction Regulations, Seaside re-created the successful elements of towns predating the automobile suburb. Houses of familiar type, materials, and style were the building blocks. The density was similar to that of the streetcar suburb, which had long been in eclipse. Seaside proved that towns with the components of traditional urbanism could be designed and built and that they could be vigorous and viable. Automobile suburbia was not the only choice.

Much credit should go to Seaside's architecture, I believe, for the successful revival of the higher density, traditionally planned, walking city. I am not suggesting that a carrot-and-stick philosophy was employed. But clearly in Seaside's early days, the architecture of its houses enjoyed tremendous appeal, though some trepidation was expressed over the sizes of the lots and the close proximity of houses to one another. After all, many buyers came from automobile suburbia and were used to that experience. In the choice of a community for their second home, they would be "getting away" to a place of higher density and closer proximity to their fellow man. This was not an easy sell. In fact, in 1982 most real estate "experts" in the Florida panhandle were convinced that Robert Davis was crazy when they heard about his plans.

The use of traditional architecture was integral to the success of Seaside. Although it hardly bears endorsement as the only form of architecture we need, its presence is a welcome addition to the contemporary urban landscape. In most aspects of our culture—government, religion, education—the present generation exists in a world steeped in tradition to which a contemporary layer is added, and then it is passed on to the next generation. But, this is not so true of the built environment. James Howard Kunstler notes in *The Geography of Nowhere* that eighty percent of everything ever built in the United States has been built since World War II. The phenomenal post-war growth has generated most of the built environment that currently exists. Communities where nothing is older than a model home built in 1963, where contemporary architecture is the only style, and where most retail establishments are chain franchises seem imbalanced. Building more traditional architecture does not solve this problem, of course, but it does help satisfy a spiritual craving to be connected to a viable past. It's like an old family recipe for vegetable soup. You may not be able to eat your great-grandmother's soup, but you can at least use her recipe. You feel part of a continuum and culturally enriched for having shared something meaningful across time.

Seaside has gone a long way toward realizing the rigorous ideals and goals of both its developer and its planners. So far, its failures have proven to be rather meager in comparison. One disappointment certainly is that, as Seaside grew, not everyone who wanted to participate was always able to do so. Economic factors increasingly determined who got in and who didn't. Expensive lot prices were further encumbered by the requirement that the owner must build within two years. Although this promoted a rapid build-out and discouraged land speculation, it meant that anyone who wanted in on the deal had to be able to afford to purchase a lot and develop it in short order. Varied lot sizes and prices, the provision for outbuildings that might house renters, and a self-sufficient town plan with enough amenities potentially to encourage many full-time residents were insufficient factors to produce true socioeconomic diversity. If town planning is capable of ensuring a broad socioeconomic cross section of humanity, it can't be proven by the experience of Seaside. Perhaps it could work in a primary-home community, but second-home communities are largely an upper-middle-class phenomenon. In any society, the second home has always been a luxury attainable only by a privileged minority. At Seaside these obstacles proved to be a greater hurdle than planning efforts could clear, at least initially.

Over time, Seaside will come to have more socioeconomic diversity than it now does. Its buildings will age. Some won't be maintained as well as others or won't be updated as frequently. Many of the current residents will retire one day and become pensioners.

Although still well-off, they won't be as financially endowed as when they were working. An even greater measure of socioeconomic diversity will occur as the residences of Seaside are inherited by the children of those who built them. As is typical in older resort towns, the houses of Seaside may come to be owned jointly by siblings, many, by then, with families of their own. What had been the proud bourgeois villa of their parents, will be the collectively owned, communally shared "old beach house," marginally maintained and left as it once was, to remind them of childhood days spent at Seaside. The next generation may look at their Seaside house differently, but also may be an altogether different class of people—less affluent and more inclined to the arts and to leisure activities. To the extent that this comes to pass, it will be the halcyon era for Seaside as a community. If and when this happens, some credit can be given to the planning effort as having come through in the long run. In the interim, it is fair to say that socially deterministic planning created a neighborly community whose residents walk and bicycle more and spend more time in the public forum than their counterparts in automobile suburbia. But socially deterministic planning did not create a community of even meager socioeconomic diversity.

The lack of socioeconomic diversity in Seaside has manifested itself in a specific way. The absence of nontransient renters, the lack of lower-middle-class homeowners, and the presence of few middle-class homeowners have made Seaside what might broadly be categorized as an upper-class resort. It is more than this, but this has become the dominant impression,

and it is increasingly seen in the residential architecture of the community. Since the late 1980s, the rule has been for the building of new houses with pretensions of being far more than modest beach cottages. Opulent beach houses like those in Newport, Rhode Island, have become pervasive prototypes. The context of Seaside does allow an appropriate and highly successful setting for grand villas on Seaside Avenue and in a few other areas of the community. Given that the ratio of patricians to plebeians is out of balance, so is the ratio of grand villas to simple cottages, in a town intended to have a more typical mix of both. The southern bungalow (type VI) has suffered the most in this squeeze. This suburban prototype with strong vernacular roots was transformed into grand villas as Seaside built out.

The bungalow-elevated-to-grand-villa is just fine as a work of architecture, but results in a "noisy" streetscape formed by too many special houses and not enough ordinary ones. Additionally, overly grand private residences siphon off interest from the public forum, which should dominate in a resort setting like Seaside's. The whole package becomes overwhelming. The overall impression is much more powerful if the individual components quietly contribute to the grandness of the whole.

As with socioeconomic diversity, time is likely to become an ally in lessening this problem. Street trees will mature, overly ambitious paint schemes of four and five colors will be repainted more conservatively in only one or two, and residents will make incremental alterations, or copy the alterations, landscaping, and color schemes of their neighbors. The streetscape will gradually become a more cohesive whole.

My first and most lasting impressions of Seaside are from a visit in August 1987 when I was beginning work on an illustrated book about cottage living in the San Francisco Bay Area. I was intrigued by the idea of a beach town made up of clapboard cottages densely nestled into the sandy, palmetto scrub of the Florida panhandle. I hoped this research would validate that my new book was exploring a lifestyle that was gathering acceptance from a wide audience seeking rustic simplicity in an urban setting.

My initial impression of Seaside, though quite positive, was tinged with some disappointments. The cottages were uniformly new. Most were bigger than I had hoped—and I was viewing Seaside before the even grander west side was developed. The houses were not as universally vernacular as I had expected they would be. Many had aspirations of grand style.

What I had expected was a tightly clustered bohemian village of beach shacks—tin roofs with rusty patches, screened porches littered with sandy floats and funky bicycles, hammocks with nearby half-read pulp fiction and half-drunk bourbon and Cokes. My vision of Seaside was of a lazy, summery place where daydreams were interrupted only by the ecstatic squeals of children playing.

Seaside's ambience was newer, its architecture somewhat grander, and life in the town more choreographed than I had expected. I nonetheless was smitten. The screened-porch dining room at Bud and Alley's Restaurant was a quintessential space. The Sip and Dip (now the Silver Bucket) ice cream parlor and sandwich shop was as appealing a beach shack as I could possibly imagine. The Savannah Pavilion was a beautiful Greek temple crafted from materials available at the local hardware on Highway 98. Even if I didn't have strong feelings for the Victorian evocations of the Rosewalk cottages, the meandering trails through the scrub, the intimate scale, and the sensitivity to the natural landscape made for a masterfully appropriate design. I concluded that with the passage of time my fantasy image of Seaside would emerge—the tin would rust, and the bicycles would become funky—and I knew that both the Gulf Coast climate and culture, which I had experienced since childhood, was capable of converting even the most industrious of Yankee souls into laid-back bohemians. The groundwork had been laid for an appropriate patina to settle over the town. Significant ideas were being realized in a new town that offered the reassurance that we, as a society, had not forgotten how to do something very important: create a compelling, stimulating, and complex place of human habitation.

These houses, which sit side by side on Tupelo Street, were the first two residences built in Seaside. Designed by Robert Davis, they are distinctive for their vernacular language and simple details. Both houses are type VI (southern bungalow). Their prototypes can readily be found in neighboring Grayton and Seagrove.

Overlooking the Gulf, near the center of Seaside's Gulf frontage, this pavilion sits atop a simple wood deck. This public building is the first built structure in Seaside. The restrained classical details contrast with the vernacular of Seaside's first two houses, just as its white paint contrasts with the polychrome siding of the houses. This pavilion is the setting for Sunday morning religious services and has been used for theatrical productions and for movie screenings on summer evenings.

TUPELO ST. FROM PAVILION

Tupelo Street, viewed from its pavilion, was the first street to be developed and is

therefore the town's most mature street in the age of its architecture, landscaping,

and infrastructure.

Development of Seaside began on the east side of the community. Rosewalk, seen from the tower of the Krier House, is a cluster of fourteen cottages nestled in dense scrub which is shared as commons—a site plan inspired by cottage courts. After Tupelo Street, Rosewalk was the next area to be developed. The houses were designed by Robert Orr and Melanie Taylor, who later established separate practices in New Haven, Connecticut. The landscaping was the work of Orr and Taylor in collaboration with Douglas Duany, Seaside's landscape designer at the time. The siting of the houses and the layout of the trails through the commons are the most organically conceived elements in the community. Orr describes the approach as "passive" in that the intent was for Rosewalk to appear to have a natural landscape rather than a manicured garden. Unlike the sandpaths throughout the rest of Seaside, the trails of Rosewalk are not defined by fences.

The Rosewalk cottages are type V category (minimal prescriptions) under the Seaside Code. A nontypical site and a minimal prescription type category for the houses resulted in a neighborhood unique within Seaside.

A bandshell sits at the end of a green on

the site of a proposed lyceum on the

west side of Seaside. In the interim, this

has become a public space for outdoor

banquets, Easter egg hunts, and

concerts. Beyond the bandshell are the

tightly clustered, tin-roofed houses of

Seaside and the town's recently

demolished water tower.

## PENSACOLA STREETSCAPE

Along Pensacola Street, a typical street perpendicular to the Gulf with type VI and VIa (southern bungalow) houses, setbacks are uniform and generous to preserve a view corridor to the Gulf. In the distance is the street's pavilion. Seaside is platted so that the views down the streets form an axis to an element of visual interest, usually architecture. This not only makes walking more interesting but also provides landmarks so pedestrians always know where they are. Any Seasider could immediately recognize and identify this streetscape by its pavilion designed by Philadelphia architect Tony Atkin.

## CADENCE OF TOWERS

Towers have come to be as integral as porches are to the Seaside house. Here, along the west side of Pensacola Street, the towers look out at other towers or provide views of the Gulf, the town, or the forest. Views of the built environment of Seaside are a coveted and decidedly urban amenity. The proliferation of towers circumvent the great deal of rhetoric that the planning of Seaside does not emphasize views.

## SANDPATHS

Complementing the streets are
sandpaths that form a pedestrian
network throughout the community. The
sandpaths allow even young children to
get around safely and independently.

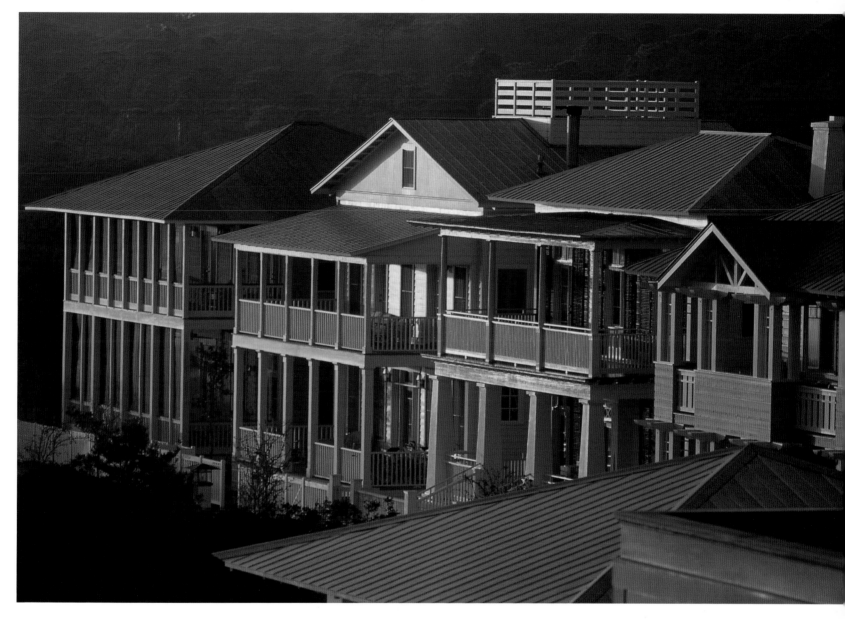

WATER TOWER PLACE

At the northwest end of Seaside is Water Tower Place, a circular drive around the former site of the town water tower. (The water tower was demolished in the fall of 1994 because its steel frame was rusting and continued maintenance was deemed too costly.) The houses are type V category which has liberal prescriptions under the code. Here substantial two-story villas with narrow yards to either side, facade-length double porches, and minimal setbacks from the street, form a cohesive urban streetscape.

## ODESSA PAVILION

The pavilions at Seaside are some of its most significant architecture. Whereas the Gulf cannot be seen from pedestrian views, the pavilions dramatically signify its presence. Monuments to the Gulf and the ritual of beachcombing, the eight pavilions currently at Seaside are separate architectural commissions, differing in design. They are the most important shared, and the most used, public amenity in Seaside.

Odessa Pavilion was designed by the late Roger Ferri, who poetically described it as "a capriccio on vernacular stick construction . . . a tropical palm-frond hut. . . . It dematerializes . . . into a flickering tent of sea and sky."

# FOREST STREET/RUSKIN PLACE PAVILION

This pavilion on the west side of the central square is one of two that will serve the residential areas behind Seaside's downtown. It is the

first, and may be the only, pavilion which will allow handicapped access on its dune walkover. It was designed by David Coleman, an

architect based in Seattle. Coleman studied in Copenhagen and based his obelisk pavilion on Scandinavian classical buildings.

## NATCHEZ PAVILION

Natchez Pavilion features a light, airy, aluminum beach umbrella at the crest of a dune walkover with railings evocative of nautical forms. It was designed and built by The Jersey Devil, a firm led by Steve Badanes. The firm's strategy is quite unusual in contemporary architecture. The customary strategy among design/build firms is for architects to design a project and then contractors to build it, each working compartmentally for the same corporation. By contrast, The Jersey Devil first creates a design and then also builds it, solving unanticipated design problems as the project evolves.

The Natchez Pavilion is the only pavilion in Seaside whose walkover is unpainted. Built of aluminum finished with marine paint and rot-resistant cedar treated with a preservative, this pavilion probably will require the least maintenance of any within the community.

## WEST SIDE PAVILIONS

Pensacola, Odessa, and Natchez pavilions, from left to right, on the west side of Seaside show how the pavilions bear little contextual relationship to one another. Each is a unique monument with its own personality.

## EAST RUSKIN PAVILION

Seasiders enjoy the sunrise at East Ruskin Pavilion, designed by Stuart Cohen and Anders Nereim. The pavilions offer elevated views that heighten the drama of the Gulf. They also provide a place for Seasiders to congregate informally. Furthermore, the walkovers protect the dunes from human trampling. The concept of the Seaside pavilions, in particular their solution to the vital issue of beach access, is integral to the success of the community.

## SAVANNAH PAVILION

Designed by Tom Christ, Savannah Pavilion is as successful as any public structure in Seaside. It possesses the simple beauty and extraordinary majesty of a Greek temple, yet was crafted with simple construction techniques and basic materials available at any local building supply.

## TUPELO PAVILION

Designed by Ernesto Buch, Tupelo Pavilion was the first pavilion built in Seaside and, since its construction in the early 1980s, has become the icon of the town. It is depicted in silhouette on brochures, note cards, posters, and placards. A twilight view of the Gulf, framed by the Tupelo Pavilion, was made into a popular poster.

## THE BEACH AS A PUBLIC FORUM

People informally congregate to sunbathe, swim, fly kites, play catch, or just relax.

It is a place where you may be alone, but not lonely. Like a lively park, plaza, or public

square, the beach is the focal point of the community.

*(opposite page)* Vacationers relax in the shade of a big beach umbrella.

## SWIM AND TENNIS CLUB

Three swimming pools in Seaside supplement the beach as a place to go for aquatic

fun and social interaction.

## DREAMLAND HEIGHTS AND MODICA MARKET

Downtown Seaside is still being developed. The Dreamland Heights building, at right, designed by New York architect Steven Holl, and the adjacent Modica Market building, by Berke and McWhorter, also of New York, were the first two downtown buildings. Both were completed in 1989.

Dreamland Heights is a four-story, mixed-use building with retail spaces on the ground floor, offices on the second floor, and residences on the top two floors. The living units on the east, or back, side were designed with certain personality archetypes in mind: The Mathematician, The Tragic Poet, The Musician—all considered "melancholic" types and given living units that face the rising sun. "Boisterous" types are located on this side of the building, facing the setting sun. The residential units in Dreamland Heights are rented for transient accommodations.

Modica Market shares the bustling arcade with Dreamland Heights. In temperate weather, large, garage-style, roll-up doors open the market to the arcade. Inside is a large open space whose prototype is the food court in Harrod's, the famed London department store, absent the Art Nouveau tile work. Modica Market, with its unpainted cinder blocks, corrugated metal awnings, and roll-up garage doors, is an elegant building that is unpretentiously straightforward about its construction.

The goal of Seaside is to be a *real* town—that is, to be as self-sufficient as possible by incorporating most of the facilities commonly found in towns: a post office, a town hall, a library, a church, and, most importantly, shops. Seaside has ambitious plans to contain fifty thousand square feet of commercial space, most of it devoted to retail.

Per-spi-cas-ity, an open-air market, is patterned after the markets common in Mediterranean towns.

Sundog Books, one of the oldest businesses in Seaside, is in its second building. Crammed floor to ceiling with a wide selection of books, it functions not just as a business, but as a place where people come to hang out and exchange ideas.

Bud and Alley's, named for a dog and a cat, was Seaside's first restaurant. The screened-porch dining room is a favorite public space. The structure is set low to the ground and nestled into the surrounding scrubby foliage. Ceiling fans purring overhead supplement the gentle Gulf breeze.

## RESIDENTIAL CLASSICISM

Originally intended for public buildings, classicism quickly crept into Seaside's residential

architecture, as in this house on West Ruskin Street.

## THE POST OFFICE

Designed by Robert Davis, the post office is a diminutive classical building in the center of

Seaside on County Road 30-A. The setting is temporary, however, as this central site is

the intended location for a public tower designed by Leon Krier. When completed, it will

be the tallest building in Seaside.

## RUSKIN PLACE

Directly behind downtown is Ruskin Place, two short blocks of town homes that face a plaza and a park. It is described as an artist's colony, though the description is more conceptual than literal, much as the term *craftsman bungalow* is used to describe a residence for a craftsman. The town houses of Ruskin Place have ground-floor studios devoted to artisanal pursuits, largely the purveying of handcrafted goods. Above these delightful shops and work spaces are residences. With masterful efficiency, a twenty-by-eighty-foot Ruskin Place lot can be developed with a building having a ground floor with as much as twelve hundred square feet of retail or studio space, a residence above of roughly double the ground-floor square footage, and a roof deck with a garden. Accessed by a service alley in the back is off-street parking for two cars.

The two center town homes were designed by New York architect Walter Chatham. They are flanked by those of another New York architect, Alexander Gorlin. They represent the style of elegant urbanity that is evolving in this Seaside neighborhood.

A patron of Studio 210, a combination coffeehouse and art gallery, admires a piece of sculpture facing the plaza.

## KRIER HOUSE

This house on Tupelo Circle designed by Leon Krier as a personal residence is notable for being the first built example of his architectural design. The roof pavilion overlooks Rosewalk and the Gulf. This house was one of the first residences painted in a monochromatic off-white color scheme. The classicism of Krier's house, combined with its location, has caused it to be appropriated as a public building. A sign on its picket fence states, "We appreciate your interest in architecture, but please do not disturb the guests." Tupelo Circle, on one side of the house, and Rosewalk, on the other, are two popular public places in the community. The majestic Greek pavilion on the roof is visible from almost every vantage point on the east side of Seaside.

Designed by New York architect Walter Chatham as a personal residence, this has become the most controversial house in Seaside. *Architectural Record* featured it as its "House of the Year" in 1989, being careful in the photography to avoid any contextual shots. It has been referred to as a dogtrot design because the two forms, actually dependent wings of the same house, are connected by a deck that functions as a dogtrot.

The interesting aspect of Chatham's house is that it conforms to many of the principles of the prototypical Seaside house. Its design is responsive to climate and its form is simple—the roof plan couldn't be simpler. The house borrows readily from vernacular predecessors and is obviously related to the prototypical beach shack, just as many other Seaside houses are, including the very ones with which it clashes.

## SEASIDE SIGNAGE

The streets that intersect County Road 30-A, like Tupelo Street, have grand signage. The markers, though restrained, are reminiscent of the gateways found at entrances to planned subdivisions in suburban neighborhoods. Traditional street signs, like this one at the intersection of Odessa and Grayton, are used within the community.

## STREET VISTAS

A view east down Grove Avenue takes in the Tupelo Circle gazebo. The street vista terminates at a point of significant architectural interest offering pedestrians and bicyclists recognizable landmarks.

BUD AND ALLEY'S RESTAURANT PAVILION

The view from beneath the pavilion at Bud and Alley's restaurant looks out to the Gulf. The pavilion, designed by David Mohney and Joan Chan, is used for outdoor dining and as a stage for entertainment on weekends.

## LITTLE SAND PINE LODGE AND WAYBACK COTTAGE

Little Sand Pine Lodge and Wayback Cottage, an adjacent guest house, were designed by Richard Gibbs, currently the Seaside Town Architect, in collaboration with designer and friend Randy Harelson. Wayback was built first, in 1987, and Little Lodge was added later, in 1990. Wayback initially served as a shared second home and is one of the best examples of the diminutive outbuildings common throughout Seaside. Little Lodge was designed as a rental property, primarily for short-term stays. The configuration of the two buildings allows a front yard for Wayback into which the main house does not encroach. Little Lodge has a rear yard that likewise is not encroached upon by the guest cottage.

Gibbs and Harelson describe the design inspiration for Wayback as essentially Caribbean, though the residence of artist Walter Anderson in the Gulf Coast town of Ocean Springs, Mississippi, was also an influence. The key prototypes for Little Sand Pine Lodge were old Florida lodges, particularly the Driftwood Inn in Vero Beach. The houses of Barbados were also influential.

Little Lodge features a roof deck that affords views of Forest Street Park in the foreground and beyond to Ruskin Place.

The screened porch off the second-floor living area overlooks the side yard and Wayback. In the background is the sand pine forest adjoining Seaside. The Adirondack porch furniture, of white cedar, consists of component parts made of two predominant forms: a half circle and a full circle. At the rear is the stair that serves as the only access between floors.

At the rear of the porch, beneath the stair and separated from the garden by blue wood louvers, is an outdoor shower for rinsing off when coming in from the beach or pool.

A bird feeder is partially concealed by an oleander. Randy Harelson, who executed the landscape design, feels that the feeder is integral to the garden because it attracts an array of birds.

A small rectangular window bay on the left side of the living area accommodates a writing desk. Awning shutters add privacy and filter the light. Their color echoes the blue of the sky and Gulf.

Little Sand Pine Lodge, named for a type of pine that exists only in the Florida panhandle, has its main living area on the second floor. This grand room features structural beams fashioned from cypress poles found in nearby Grayton Beach. The flooring is yellow pine, and the ceiling is of the same wood, left unfinished. The central metal stair accesses a roof deck. The living room furniture is an assemblage of pieces collected over the years. The antlers adorning the wall reinforce the lodge influence. The painted wood figures above the windows on the right are by local artist Chick Huettel.

The front bedroom is accessed through the door on the ground-floor porch. The entry to the bathroom is at left. Each of the two bedrooms has its own bath. There is no internal connection between the bedrooms, making them secluded from one another. The placement of highly privatized bedrooms downstairs and an open communal room upstairs enforces the image and function of the house as a lodge.

On the left wall is a linoleum cut by Gulf Coast artist Walter Anderson. The artwork above the bedside table is a woodcut of the lighthouse in Biloxi, Mississippi, by Randy Harelson's brother Clint. The louvered wood shutters open in bifold fashion to fit the spaces alongside the windows, an arrangement replicated upstairs. The cedar furniture matches the pieces on the porch.

On either side of the bathroom lavatory are wall-mounted torchères designed by Randy Harelson, with stems made of cypress knees. These fixtures were inspired by those in the dining room of the Island Hotel in Cedar Key, Florida. The cabinet has a maple countertop, just like the counters in the kitchen.

In Wayback Cottage, the bedroom is on the second floor. Shuttered French doors open out to a small porch. The hip roof of the porch conceals from public view a window air-conditioning unit punched through the gable. This economical solution saved the expense of a central system. The walls are unfinished yellow pine, and the ceiling is plywood, painted white with a slight aqua tint. Gypsum wallboard is not used in this house or Little Lodge. All the furnishings in the room, including the artwork, were retrieved from the attic of Harelson's mother in Baton Rouge, Louisiana.

**WAYBACK COTTAGE**
OWNERS  *Richard Gibbs and Randy Harelson*
ARCHITECTS  *Richard Gibbs with Randy Harelson*
DATE  *Completed in 1987*
CONTRACTOR  *Benoit Laurent, Laurent Construction*

**LITTLE SAND PINE LODGE**
OWNERS  *Richard Gibbs and Randy Harelson*
ARCHITECTS  *Richard Gibbs with Randy Harelson*
DATE  *Completed in 1990*
CONTRACTOR  *Benoit Laurent, Laurent Construction*

# PLEASURE PRINCIPAL

Pleasure Principal is an informal collaboration between two San Francisco architects, Jeremy Kotas and Paul "Skip" Shaffer, who used the rather whimsical name, Acme Romance, to identify their design alliance. Kotas is a principal at Kotas/Pantaleoni. Before establishing his own practice, he worked at MLTW and later in the Los Angeles office of Frank Gehry. Shaffer established an architectural practice in San Francisco after moving from Los Angeles when he received a commission to design a house at Anchor Bay, near Sea Ranch. This is the one Seaside house, to date, designed by architects whose work experience includes participation in substantial commissions at, or near, Sea Ranch. It is also distinctive in that it was commissioned by the author.

Seen from both street and sandpath-fronting elevations, the house is intended to be somewhat ambiguous in its hierarchy of front to side elevations. The intended perception in both instances is that you are looking at the front of the house.

The exterior view looking west, taken before the house on the adjacent lot was constructed, shows the relationship between the house's tower and Seaside's former water tower. The placement of the columns describes a cylinder, a subtle acknowledgment of the form of the water tower. The house tower is patterned after the U.S. Forestry Department fire towers used throughout the Southeast.

Pleasure Principal, a variation on the dogtrot house, has front and rear modules spanned by a screened porch. Stylistically, the house owes a great deal to rural industrial structures like equipment sheds. These structures proved to be interesting prototypes since the materials from which they are commonly constructed—corrugated metal, wood siding, and unadorned wooden pillars—have been in continuous use. This approach made the house seem more contemporary and not a "revival."

From the street entrance, the side porch opens up to a grand dogtrot that separates the kitchen and living room on the ground floor. A mezzanine spans the porch and connects the two second-floor bedrooms. The only stair is located on the porch. Architects Kotas and Shaffer describe this space as "a great outdoor room." Their design philosophy was to use the porch as both the grand architectural space of the house and the central corridor of circulation. This strategy provides many functional benefits and, because porches are inexpensive to construct, satisfied budgetary constraints while offering architectural drama. The dogtrot effectively expands what is a small house—1,040 square feet of interior space—allowing it to assume proportions more in keeping with its neighbors.

The rear bedroom looks across the dogtrot to the street. The porch has proven integral to beach living at Pleasure Principal: It is a repository for sandy floats, chairs, and beach toys. It allows direct access to bathrooms so that water and sand from the beach are not

tracked into other rooms. It provides additional separation and privacy for the two bedrooms, important in vacation homes, where friends and relatives who don't ordinarily live together may vacation together. Finally, it aids immensely in the cross-ventilation of the house. The central air-conditioning system, installed when the house was built, seldom needs to be used. Traditionally, it was always considered antithetical to air-condition Gulf beach cabins.

The kitchen is a galley inspired by the efficient cooking arrangements in boats and commercial kitchens. For large groups, the dining table is used for food preparation and serving, while the meal is usually held on the picnic table on the porch. Open shelves nearly reach the twelve-foot ceilings. Higher shelves are for mementos. The radio on the top right shelf survived a hurricane at a relative's cabin in the early 1970s. It was found unscathed, amid the debris, and serves as a good luck charm against future hurricanes. A plate rail accommodates a combination of functional objects and mementos. Honest and affordable materials are used in undisguised fashion throughout the house: vinyl composition floor tiles, plywood for shelving, walls, and upstairs floors, gypsum board for ceilings. It was felt that these materials would make the house seem durable and promote an enjoyment of the house rather than a preoccupation with protecting delicate finishes.

This view from the kitchen across the dogtrot to the living room shows how the plan offers many of the benefits of a loft plan without some of the disadvantages. Clusters of activity in the communal spaces are accommodated well. Children can play in the dogtrot, while adults can engage in a card game on the dining table or converse in the living room, all with marginal cross-interference.

The Gulf breeze flows easily through the front bedroom and the rest of the house. This room is quite small, so it does not have a traditional closet with doors. A partition behind the double bed serves as a headboard, a surface for reading lights, and a central niche that accommodates a phone. Behind the partition on either side are poles from which clothes can be hung and remain shielded from view. Indirect lighting is also concealed behind this multipurpose partition. The photograph above the bed is of the landscape at Eden State Park near Seaside.

In keeping with our concept of farm buildings as prototypes, we decided that what we were creating was a modern farmhouse, that is, a traditional country house, more restrained stylistically and more vernacular than a similar urban type and modern only in a provincial sense. Pleasure Principal is about what Robert Venturi called "ugly and ordinary" architecture. I describe it in less polemical terms as "plain and typical." Kotas and Shaffer call it "plainstyle." Pleasure Principal is an example of how the Seaside Urban Code functions as a type code. The Charleston, side-yard house, the prescribed type for this lot, was almost always styled in the classic-romantic tradition, not in the vernacular. The dogtrot, the most distinctive feature of Pleasure Principal, was not intrinsic to the prototype.

PLEASURE PRINCIPAL

OWNERS  *Richard and Rives Sexton*

ARCHITECTS  *Jeremy Kotas and Skip Shaffer,*
*Acme Romance*

DATE  *Completed in 1990*

CONTRACTOR  *Mark Breaux,*
*Breaux Construction*

Forsythe House, completed in 1990, was the first row house of Ruskin Place, just to the north of Seaside's downtown. The intent of Ruskin Place has been fully realized in the residence of Bill and Mary Florence Forsythe, designed by architect Walter Chatham. The Forsythes were drawn to Chatham because they admired the sensibilities of his residence on East Ruskin Street.

A simple constructed quality prevails both on the exterior and in the interior finishes and fixtures. A small garden of flowering plants softens the facade. The French doors and transoms are protected from the elements by roll-up canvas shades that can be tied down with cleats when the house is left vacant. The balcony, a basic design of galvanized steel construction, was inspired by the fire escapes of New York City lofts.

A heavy-duty restaurant stove is surrounded by metro shelves which are creatively cluttered with functional kitchen utensils and mementos.

Separated from the dining room by the central stairs, the kitchen is a two-story volume with an industrial ambience. Mary Florence formerly ran a catering business, and this influenced the down-to-basics, functional attitude that guided layout and aesthetics. The table is fashioned from a four-by-eight sheet of industrial steel, sandblasted and then mounted to table legs. The countertops are concrete poured into a steel mold. The light fixtures, used in indirect configurations throughout the house, are castoffs from a dance studio. Commercial fans overhead provide a cooling breeze in the summer.

The stairway walls are a battleship gray base sponged with aluminum paint, a technique improvised by Mary Florence. Industrial cables held taut with turnbuckles form a balustrade for the stair. The cinder-block walls are painted white. Bill describes them as "gritty" like the beach environment. (Inexpensive cinder-block construction was common in post–World War II beach cabins in the area.) The floors are porcelain tile, a material that the Forsythes found to be the most resistant to the abrasiveness of sand.

Custom cabinets can be rolled out from both ends of the counter to expose the chopping blocks on top. The units are constructed of persimmon wood scavenged from a fallen tree in the yard of the Forsythes' contractor. Impressed with the unusual grain of the wood, they had these cabinet fronts made from it.

The dining room on the first floor opens to Ruskin Place. This is where Mary Florence Forsythe and her daughter Sarah conduct art classes for adults and children. The dining table is a converted seamstress table that Bill Forsythe painted in a checkerboard pattern. The chairs are old director's chairs refreshed with new striped covers. Much like Mary Florence's approach to art, recycling old industrial objects for a new purpose and setting is a recurring theme in this house. In the background on the left are a mirror and lamps by artist Chester Old from the "Form Meets Function" exhibit at Seaside. On the right is a functional sculpture in concrete and steel by Mary Florence.

The clawfoot tub in the upstairs bathroom had been residing in the attic of the Forsythes' contractor awaiting a new life. A stainless steel basket that formerly served a nautical purpose now holds toilet paper. Additional items are stored in the hanging galvanized bucket.

Directly above the living room is one of two bedrooms. The columns flanking the bed, from a plantation house near Tallahassee, are cypress with plaster capitals. All the lamps are by Mary Florence, as is the steel chair in the background. The vanity is fashioned from two steel pillars retrieved from a junkyard. The countertop is made from the excess steel from the sheet used for the kitchen table. As in the living room below, a screen of rubberized drapery liner, hanging by shower curtain rings from a metal cable, can be closed to give the space privacy. A similar treatment is used on all the French doors in the house. The transom hopper windows rest against the curtain cable when opened.

The living room is on the second floor facing Ruskin Place. The coffee table, the work of Mary Florence, has legs of concrete cast with Seaside foliage pressed against it to form fossil-like impressions. The sofa, in a copper-finish vinyl, is flanked in the foreground by one of Mary Florence's copper lamps and in the background by a lamp from New Orleans designer Mario Villa. The welded sheet-metal piece on the wall is by Mary Florence. The knobs for the closets in the house are improvised from thick sisal rope tied into knots.

The two-story kitchen and the bedroom above are visible from the rear of the house. Parking is provided for two cars, and a heating and air-conditioning unit is hidden from view by an enclosure. These town homes are the most land-efficient residences in Seaside. The standard lot size is a remarkable twenty feet by eighty feet.

FORSYTHE HOUSE
**OWNERS**  *Bill and Mary Florence Forsythe*
**ARCHITECT**  *Walter Chatham*
**DATE**  *Completed in 1990*
**CONTRACTOR**  *Mike Warner, Warnerworks*

# OVERBOARD!

Overboard! is a four-building compound formed by the main house shown here, the annex behind it, and, behind the main house, a small, two-story cottage and a utility building. Together these buildings form the Seaside "estate" of David Dowler. The complex was a collaboration between architect Rafael Pelli, a partner in the firm Cesar Pelli & Associates in New Haven, Connecticut, and Nonya Grenader, an architect based in Houston. Pelli was primarily responsible for the overall design program, and Grenader handled the details such as working drawings and interior details.

The communal rooms are on the second floor. The living room has French doors that open out to the facade-length screened porch. The walls here and throughout the compound are horizontal tongue-and-groove pine with pronounced gaps that impart a rustic quality. The floors are oak, stained in a provincial finish. The tiles on the fireplace surround and hearth are by ceramicist Claudia Reese of Austin, Texas. Above the fireplace is a Sally Mann photograph titled *Sorry*, named for the game her children are playing. The two children's Adirondack chairs are from the store at the Whitney Museum of American Art. The sofas are from Pallazetti and the wicker chair is by Larsen Loom. In the background on the left is a Sid Avery photograph of Audrey Hepburn from 1957 and on the right a 1955 photograph by Louise Dahl-Wolfe titled *Twins at the Beach*. David Dowler is an avid art collector; the emphasis of his collection is photography.

The southwest corner of the screened porch offers a shady spot for reading and taking in the vista down Odessa Street. The wicker furniture, by Larsen Loom, was chosen because it resembles the wicker used on the porch of the old family beach house at Laguna Beach, a few miles east of Seaside, where Dowler spent summers during his childhood.

The kitchen, separated from the living room by the stairs, opens to the dining area. The island countertop is custom Corian. Fixtures with brushed finishes were chosen throughout because they resemble the patinated finish on old fixtures. The tile on the background counter is by Claudia Reese.

A window looks from the small third-floor sitting room to the dining room. The large round table is very flexible in the number of diners who can be seated intimately. There are no window coverings on the windows in the dining room or throughout most of the compound. The exception is where the need for privacy dictates the use of a window covering. In these instances, simple wood miniblinds are used. The intent was to flood the house with light. The off-white walls enhance the sense of abundant sunlight.

The first floor of the main house has two bedrooms. The cypress furniture in the master bedroom was made by Dietlein, Inc., following the designs of Acadian and Creole furniture traditions of south Louisiana. The elegant simplicity of this furniture makes it a fine choice for a refined beach house.

The annex includes a communal room designed for watching television, listening to music, or playing cards. The only television in the compound is in the annex. The module that holds the television also houses speakers and electronic components. Behind this unit is a half bath and wet bar. A captain's ladder on the right accesses a sleeping loft.

Overboard! is distinctive for several reasons. In spite of allocating a generous budget that could have resulted in an ostentatious house, Dowler opted for a complex of buildings on two lots which are in scale with their neighbors. The various buildings are held together by a coherent arrangement on the site and by connecting boardwalks. Equally important as a unifying element is the consistent use of finishes, fixtures, appliances, and furniture. Architectural restraint was essential in ensuring that this grand complex did not overpower its surroundings. Overboard! is rare within Seaside, a pronounced departure from the prescribed code requirements for the two lots on which it sits. Nonetheless, it blends in harmoniously and helps form, with neighboring Butler Street facades, a uniform streetscape.

OVERBOARD!
**OWNER** *David Dowler*
**ARCHITECTS** *Rafael Pelli and Nonya Grenader*
**DATE** *Completed in 1992*
**CONTRACTOR** *Mike Warner, Warnerworks*

SUNSET AT SEASIDE

Bathed in the afterglow of twilight are the Pensacola, Odessa, and Natchez pavilions and the six Honeymoon Cottages designed by

former Seaside town architect Scott Merrill. Altogether there are twelve Honeymoon Cottages in Seaside. Another six, sited as these are,

flank East Ruskin Pavilion on the other side of town. The Honeymoon Cottages, designed for short romantic sojourns at the beach, are

rented to couples unaccompanied by children. The upper porches offer unobstructed Gulf views. Below each is a hot tub that can be

closed off with canvas curtains. A twilight wedding at one of Seaside's pavilions, followed by a stay in a Honeymoon Cottage, has

become a popular matrimonial rite.

SUNSET FROM
PENSACOLA PAVILION

Seasiders gather on Thanksgiving Day to witness the sun setting into the Gulf. Seconds

later they burst into applause as the Gulf swallows the last orange sliver and twilight

begins to envelop the town.

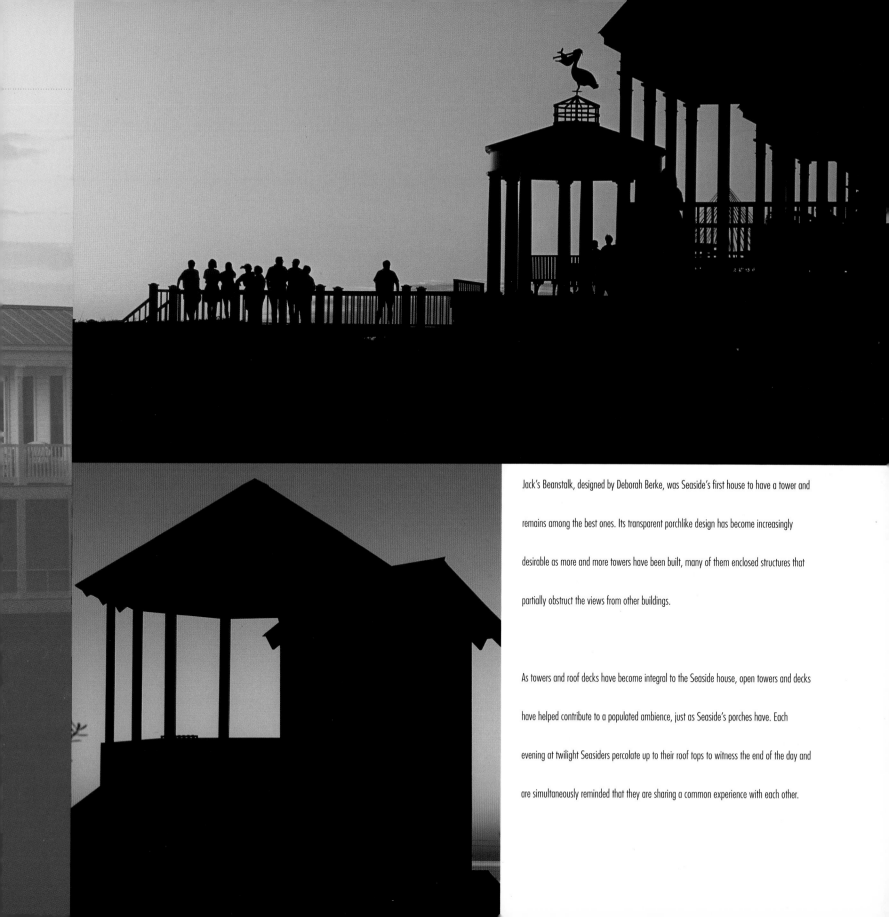

Jack's Beanstalk, designed by Deborah Berke, was Seaside's first house to have a tower and remains among the best ones. Its transparent porchlike design has become increasingly desirable as more and more towers have been built, many of them enclosed structures that partially obstruct the views from other buildings.

As towers and roof decks have become integral to the Seaside house, open towers and decks have helped contribute to a populated ambience, just as Seaside's porches have. Each evening at twilight Seasiders percolate up to their roof tops to witness the end of the day and are simultaneously reminded that they are sharing a common experience with each other.

# Prospects for

## C O M M U N I T Y

RAY OLDENBURG

Americans, observed Jean Paul Sartre, are dying of loneliness.

The collective efforts and mutual sacrifice that bound us together during World War II are but fading memories. We are lonely in our crowds and live an isolated life in our suburbs. Visitors to our country sense the death of community, here, in the unhappy faces that fill our airports, line our coffee counters, and depress our subway cars. Our disassociation from one another is evident in the growing imbalance between a shared and public life and an acquisitional and privatized one.

So pronounced has been the shift toward privatized lifestyles that the American Dream has been sorely reshaped. Gone, observes professor of architecture and urban planning Dolores Hayden, is the ideal of community so crucial to our establishment as a nation and so essential to our predecessors' well-being and contentment. It has been replaced by the dream of an ideal house, which has since become more of an escape from community than a connection to it. Never before, says Hayden, has the vision of a people focused on anything so small as a house.

The decline of community has been a perennial theme in American social commentary for most of this century, but only recently has bad community planning gotten the blame it so richly deserves. The deficiencies in our built environment have come under heavy attack by both architects and users.

Interest in projects like Sea Ranch and Seaside, therefore, goes much deeper than a mere "new look" in housing. These and several less publicized ventures are part of a radical departure from the planning and development that has fostered the isolation and atomization of our postwar population. Visitors to Seaside and Sea Ranch have a grander curiosity than those visiting the typical developers' annual "Parade of Homes." They are interested in much more than innovations in the dinette or enlarged bathrooms. They look to these places for signs of the rebirth of community in America.

When mass production of the automobile began, its chief producer boasted that it would make possible a form of community life combining the best of the city and the best of country living. The automobile came in overwhelming numbers, but the blessed combination eluded us. The automobile suburb has not put people amid natural surroundings, and it avails no one of the rich diversity of relationships and experiences inherent in large cities. The typical suburb built after World War II lacks the advantages of both city and country life far more than it incorporates them.

Seaside and Sea Ranch deserve careful attention as significant departures from Henry Ford's failed illusion. Seaside, its captivating natural setting notwithstanding, is very much an experiment in the New Urbanism. It inclines toward the city with amenities where people may live together and not merely close to one another. Sea Ranch rejects the individualized vest-pocket gardening of the subdivision in a bona fide return to nature wherein even the houses may not intrude against natural beauty. There, stewardship of the land is the first requirement of citizenship, and peoples' relationships with nature is at least as important as those with their neighbors. And, as we have seen, both communities bring people together far more successfully than the ubiquitous suburb that presently dominates the settled landscape.

Ford was not necessarily wrong in his vision of the kinds of communities that automobile transportation would make possible.

What he did not anticipate was that, in American city planning, cars would become more important than people. Acceptance of the automobile did not necessitate the policies that accompanied it. Unifunctional planning, the surrender of the streets to the cars, and the residential sterility imposed by negative zoning were largely avoidable. The automobile merely made possible the kind of planning that has been disastrous to both our cities and our neighborhoods.

Such was not the case initially. Until the late 1920s, when the automobile was already very much with us, community building in the United States was very successful, so much so, in fact, that the New Urbanism looks to those old neighborhoods for guidance and proclaims that the future does not have to be imagined so much as remembered.

Unfortunately, the Great Depression put a virtual halt to community building for many years. Construction resumed in explosive proportions after World War II, but without the wisdom to retain the best of what American tradition had to offer. The pervasive modes of residential development were anticommunity in their very design. A building binge on a scale no living American will ever see again gave Americans the largest houses on the largest lots of any country in the world. But it did so in a manner echoing the assessment of the nation's cities by the chief architect of Warsaw's postwar reconstruction, Adolf Ciborowski—communities were destroyed in the very process of being built.

Disenchantment with the quality of life and the alienating conditions in these developments was inevitable and predictable, but long in coming. As we seek alternatives to the automobile suburb, we should remember that we once regarded these places as the shining alternative to urban conditions in the 1940s.

The inner cities had deteriorated to the point where their "magnetic polarity" was reversed. Successful cities are vital and attractive, day and night. In them, the middle class and particularly the upper middle class seek housing as close to "the action" as possible. They prefer to live near the cafés, opera houses, theaters, symphony halls, arenas, specialty shops, museums, restaurants, etc., which make urban life exciting. But few cities in postwar America held such allure. Most of them encourage the highly publicized middle-class flight to the suburbs.

In contrast to the unsightliness, noise, and dangers blighting the inner cities, the typical subdivision looked attractive. Rows of sameness devoid of any centers of interest nonetheless provided an ordered tranquillity, a quiet relief from the noisy congestion of an automobile-choked city.

Symbolic and psychological motivations reinforced aesthetic ones. Impersonal and often monotonous and stressful work settings, coupled with an inhospitable urban environment, increased the desire for quiet and comfortable escape. The house became, for most, the only place of relaxation, and only houses were allowed in the new residential areas.

Little more than the size and price of housing varied, for everywhere in the new developments the "stuff of community" was absent—banned by municipal ordinance. The typical resident of postwar housing lives in what may be called a "nothing neighborhood." Nothing exists within walking distance, and in many developments there aren't any sidewalks to walk upon. There is nothing that requires neighborhood participation and nothing, usually, that even invites it. There is nothing to hold people upon retirement, nothing for the kids to do, no place to meet and get acquainted with neighbors.

There are some people who prefer to live like hermits, as Karl Hess once observed, but the subdivisions are built as if everyone wants to live that way. Why should American residential communities have been so designed? Historian Christopher Lasch has argued that such planning cannot rest on the claim that it promotes a sense of community. It rests, rather, "on a critique of community— on the claim that small towns and city neighborhoods are narrow, ethnocentric, suspicious of outsiders, and intolerant of 'difference'. . . ." This view is generally associated with postmodern intellectualism, and its proponents typically argue for community almost everywhere but where it's most needed—where children grow up and where marriages and families need indigenous social support.

But a wider, less articulated base of support for "nothing neighborhoods" is found in the ideal of "togetherness," one of the worst notions ever to capture the American middle-class imagination. The idea is that if couples or families do some things together, they should do virtually everything together. From such a perspective, community ceases to be necessary and may even interfere with "togetherness."

Of course, couples should enjoy as much togetherness as suits them, just as the small town offered as much community as one wanted. In the case of marriage and family life, however, zoning had the effect of forcing togetherness on every marriage and family living under its dictates. If one considers the countless subdivisions containing nothing but houses and wonders what kinds of relationships are provided for here, the answer is immediately obvious—only those contained within the houses.
And how has the forced togetherness that replaced a wider involvement with neighbors worked out? Divorce rates have never

been higher than in postwar America. As never before, Americans are postponing marriage or avoiding it altogether. Marriage is increasingly seen as a trap and also a relationship not likely to last.

The forced togetherness imposed in the subdivisions also explains an otherwise curious American phenomenon. As we've already noted, Americans have the largest houses in the world. Yet, we seem intent on making them even larger. We convert garages to living space and park cars outside. We close in back patios and convert basements to gain more living space. We add rooms, even entire wings, to our houses to gain more living space.

There are two reasons for this, the lesser one being to contain the paraphernalia of recreation and entertainment which we invest in heavily to compensate for the lack of shared recreation in the neighborhood. The overequipped house in the underequipped neighborhood makes for an expensive lifestyle.

But the greater reason Americans go to considerable expense to increase their living space is to escape from the family. We live in neighborhoods that offer no escape. A stroll down to the corner which brought our grandparents the relief of lighthearted company takes us nowhere. A neighborhood which doesn't even offer people a chance to "get out of the house" is a sorry one indeed.

The late social historian Philippe Ariés was invited to our shores to present a paper at a 1976 symposium on the "crisis in the family" in America. He contended that the crisis was not with the family but with the city, that in the absence of those relationships which once made the city and provided a supporting context for family life, "the role of the family overexpanded like a hypertrophied cell" as it tried to take up the slack. The costly expansions of domestic living space to relieve the cabin fever of modern marriage and family life demonstrate the wisdom in Ariés's diagnosis.

Adolescents, of course, "bust out" of the too small world of households situated in "nowheresville," and because there's no place for them in the neighborhoods, parents are left to worry about where they are, what they're doing, and, most of all, whether they are safe. Many nightmare years now attend the raising of children, and about one couple in six at the present time is resolved not to have children at all. The future of family life in this country may well depend upon the creation of a supportive community in which it may be embedded.

Under "togetherness planning," people can get together with neighbors only in the privacy of their homes. This restriction, as author Jane Jacobs so clearly understood, makes people "exceedingly choosy as to who their neighbors are or whom they associate with at all." The "all or nothing" imperative discourages association. It greatly shrinks the worlds of those in the subdivisions. People who do not know small towns often fear them for this very reason. What they fail to understand is that small towns provided many kinds of relationships that neither demanded nor encouraged "togetherness." These relationships, in turn, were made possible by the many public places providing casual and unencumbering sociability.

Ariés adored the nineteenth century for this very reason. Its cafés and cabarets offered a public counterbalance to the increasing isolation or privatization of domestic life. In such places, association with both strangers and people from different walks of life was easy, informative, and entertaining. An engaging informal public life

afforded people a personal, conversational connection to the larger society. Postwar zoning eliminated these essential gathering places or assigned them to remote locations, thus nullifying their community-building function.

Against this backdrop of anticommunity residential development, the innovations at Seaside and Sea Ranch are laudable indeed. Each project, in its own way, subordinates individual houses to a greater communal context without subtracting from their comforts and conveniences. Each makes possible a good deal of living beyond the domicile, away from television, and yet very close by. Each offers family members connection to other people with whom association is easy, and which does not necessitate invading the privacy of the home. And, in each case, one may anticipate the emergence of a distinctive local culture and that sense of place so sorely lacking in subdivisions.

At Sea Ranch and Seaside, in contrast to the automobile suburb, the stage is set for community. Each invites shared activity and provides ample common space. Good stage design, however, does not ensure a good play. What might be called the "Swedish paradox" illustrates this point. In urbanized Sweden, public areas are abundant, well maintained, and inviting. The amenities have been provided, but there is very little public life, and people retreat to their homes much as people do in our suburbs.

The acid test of community, and the common denominator in all its many definitions, is interaction. Are people engaging one another in conversation regularly and often? Here is the most certain measure of a community's vitality, and it is usually called "sociability." Sociability is of two basic kinds, pure and incidental. Pure sociability occurs when people gather for the sole purpose of enjoying one another's company. Incidental sociability occurs when people enjoy being and talking with one another in the context of goal-oriented activity such as working, traveling, running errands, or shopping.

There is no mistaking that both kinds of sociability, pure and incidental, have depended upon the existence of local commercial establishments in America's towns and cities. Pure sociability was engaged at the soda fountain in the local drugstore, the neighborhood candy store, the corner tavern, or the coffee counter at the local bakery or diner. Such places were coopted by locals who met at them regularly and counted on doing so.

Incidental sociability attended each trip to the corner grocery, or the local butcher, barber, baker, hardware store, post office, or bank. Shopping, once a chore, was made interesting and pleasurable because news and gossip were exchanged, not just money and goods, and because people dealt with one another as persons, not just customers and clerks. And importantly, in walking from one's residence to local business places, one met others on the street and at least maintained speaking acquaintance with them.

Unfortunately, the success of America's burgeoning corporate chains depends upon killing off local commercial establishments, and they have been highly successful at doing so. Retailing that once contributed so much to community life has largely been replaced by retailing that does not. The money that the chains siphon out of an area is not the only loss to the people who live there.

Chain operations could not have achieved their behemoth proportions had zoning not prohibited commercial establishments in residential developments. The low-volume, steady-state, small businesses, which were truly "convenience" stores and at which "everybody knew your name," appealed to many. Zoning resulted in the higher volumes of trade necessary to the chains. Zoning effectively herds people from miles around into the malls, strips, and shopping centers where only the corporations can afford to rent retail space.

The purging of residential neighborhoods of not only small retail operations but also anything that might amuse, attract, or merely bring people into contact with one another also favors the chains. The resulting boredom and lifelessness of the neighborhood prompt people to escape it. And where is there to go? Most find that the urban landscape seems to contain little more than the malls, the strips, and the shopping centers.

The relationship between local commercial establishments and neighborhood sociability is very strong, but neither may sound all that compelling to the prospective American house buyer. There is another consideration, however, which is closely related to them both and which is compelling. It is the factor of convenience.

Postwar America is probably the most inconvenient nation in the world. It is a fact that the places Americans must routinely visit are more scattered than in any other country and that we regularly have to drive greater distances than anyone else. It is also a fact that we have to get into an automobile for virtually everything we need as there is nothing within walking distance. The misnamed and ridiculously expensive "convenience store" suggests the very inconvenience imposed upon residential neighborhoods. If it were really convenient, one wouldn't have to drive to get to it.

The inconvenience imposed on our residential areas takes a greater and greater toll as time goes by. When the wife and mother could afford to stay home, American marriages enjoyed a division of labor that was reasonably efficient. Now, however, most wives are employed outside the home, and those households typically suffer both stress and fatigue. Nobody seems to be "on top of" housework anymore.

Seaside's reliance upon local commercial establishments is obvious from the briefest visit. It is possible that communities such as Sea Ranch will foster sociability without convenient commercial enterprises, but, if so, two problems will remain. First, living there will not be all that convenient. People will have to "pack in" supplies, make careful shopping lists, and be quite strategic about securing the necessities of daily life. Second, they will necessarily have to use their automobiles more than would otherwise be necessary. The greater the number of automobiles about, the greater their collective ugliness and the greater the danger they pose, especially to children. Also, there is no being sociable with people passing by in cars.

In the south part of Walton County, where Seaside is located, the citizens are holding meetings to make democratic decisions about how this largely undeveloped part of the county should be planned. All they could agree on initially is that they didn't want their county to be like another to the east of them which is filled with automobile congestion and the intrusive, competing logos of the corporate chains.

Perhaps before long, the "nothing neighborhoods" begat by negative zoning and applauded by the corporations that have developed

them and by those who feed off their sterility will become the negative example. Perhaps citizens and planners and developers will soon be sitting down and agreeing, first of all, that they don't want "one of those lifeless suburbs." America has tried them, and found them wanting.

Two things seem particularly encouraging at this juncture. The first concerns the marketplace where community innovations either catch on or die. Here, the evidence to date is most favorable. Given a choice, people are paying more to live in neighborhoods with diversity and convenience, and with people in the streets, than they are paying to live in quiet sterility.

The second positive sign concerns user "input." The "nothing neighborhoods" were, for the most part, built when city planners wielded absolute power and ordinary citizens had none. They were built, moreover, when the public was woefully illiterate in matters pertaining to the built environment. As former *Washington Post* architecture critic Wolf Von Eckardt once put it, the average American knew more about how a wren builds its nest than about how human habitats were constructed. All of this has undergone tremendous changes in recent years. User involvement in environmental planning is, in many places, showing the way back to grass roots democracy in America.

A final comment is in order about the idea of community. When the automobile, the streetcar, and the elevated train became commonplace in America, many observers applauded the advent of "easy transportation." For the first time in history, they felt, people were freed from locality. They could escape narrow provincialism and cultivate more desirable relationships in a wider, more cosmopolitan world. Subsequently, there appeared many new definitions of community which excluded home and neighborhood altogether. Locality became not merely unimportant but an evil to overcome. At its best, locality came to be seen as a pleasant physical setting for the privatized home, uncluttered and to be used for no other purposes.

One of the more important lessons of the past half century of constructing human habitat is that we can never be free of locality. If it is sterile, there will be a corresponding emptiness in our lives. If it is narrowly segregated by income, we will not know democracy. If its remoteness makes marriage and family life stressful, marriages and families will suffer real consequences. If it does not offer contact with many different kinds of people, human development will be retarded at all ages. If it is isolating, we will be lonely.

However their many visitors ultimately judge Seaside and Sea Ranch, both projects should at least be appreciated for having met the first requirement of a residential community: both give their residents ample reasons to walk down their own streets and pathways. And when people do that, they find each other.

## 1850 ~ 1950
### THE FORMATION of the INDUSTRIAL ANTI-CITY
### (INDUSTRIAL CITY = CONTRADICTIO in TERMINI)

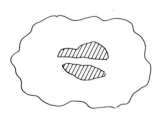

INDUSTRIAL SUB URB.
BAN LIEU · FAU BOURG
VOR ORT ·
SATELLITES · TRABANTEN
BESIEGE
the CITY

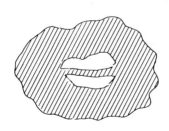

The CITY is
FINE
WITHOUT SUB URB

SUB~URB
UNTHINKABLE

WITHOUT the CITY

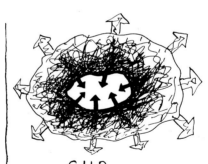

SUB URBS
FIRST
DESTROY the

LANDSCAPE & FORESTS
AND THEN
the
CITY

*—Courtesy Leon Krier*

I gratefully acknowledge the many individuals who contributed significantly to this project. For giving generously of their time and knowledge during interviews with me, I thank the following: the developer of Seaside, Robert Davis, who consented to multiple interviews and helped answer every question that arose concerning Seaside; architectural historian and writer Sally Woodbridge and the late planning consultant and architectural writer Jim Burns, both of whom have followed the Sea Ranch story since its early days; landscape architect and planner Lawrence Halprin and architects Joseph Esherick, William Turnbull, Jr., and Donlyn Lyndon, all of whom played key design roles at Sea Ranch and openly shared their intimate knowledge of this experience; planner Andres Duany who, in collaboration with his wife Elizabeth Plater-Zyberk, planned Seaside and who enthusiastically offered numerous insights on their approach to planning communities; architect Robert Orr who, in collaboration with former partner Melanie Taylor, designed Rosewalk, an early and influential component of Seaside; architects Jeremy Kotas and Skip Shaffer who were very helpful in sharing their unique perspective gained from their involvement in commissions at both Sea Ranch and Seaside;  former Seaside town architect, Scott Merrill, and current Seaside town architect, Richard Gibbs, for sharing their experiences; Seaside building inspector John Seaborn for his help with the Seaside map on page 105; architect Jeffrey Teel for his informative tours of Sea Ranch and crucial feedback and leads during the formative stages of this project; architect Ted Smith, the Sea Ranch Director of Planning and Design, who provided considerable information about the particulars of the design process at Sea Ranch; Janann Strand, a longtime Sea Ranch resident, who shared many of her personal experiences and insights on Sea Ranch as a community; Jim and Mary Alinder, full-time Sea Ranch residents, who offered insight to their experiences there; Kevin Keim of Moore/Andersson Architects, personal assistant to the late Charles Moore, who was very helpful in the coordination of photography and review of factual information concerning Moore's condominium at Sea Ranch; architect Xavier Iglesias of DPZ for review of factual information regarding the planning of Seaside; architect Obie Bowman who provided helpful information regarding his projects at Sea Ranch; and all the participants in the Posh Squash Garden, the community garden at Sea Ranch, for openly sharing their experiences with me.

I thank both Ray Oldenburg and William Turnbull, Jr., (again) for contributing insightful essays that dramatically expanded the scope of this book.

For graciously allowing me to photograph the interiors of their homes, I thank Ed and Kathleen Anderson, David Dowler, Richard Gibbs and Randy Harelson, Bill and Mary Florence Forsythe, Tom Haines and Karin Swanson, Charles Moore, and Jeffrey and Brenda Teel.

For helping with the coordination of photography at Seaside, I thank everyone at the Seaside Cottage Rental Agency. Additionally, I thank Craig Macaluso, who assisted me with the photography in Seaside, and Jim Grove, who assisted with the photography at Sea Ranch.

I thank Jeffrey and Brenda Teel, again, for the particular contribution of being such wonderful hosts during the time I spent in Sea Ranch working on this book.

I thank Leon Krier for allowing me to include several of his drawings which so graphically illustrate issues of the built environment. Additionally, I thank Louisiana artist Douglas Bourgeois and the Arthur Roger Gallery in New Orleans for allowing me to reproduce the painting *The Development,* and aerial photographer and author Alex MacLean for allowing me to reproduce one of his aerial views of Seaside.

I thank my editor at Chronicle Books, William LeBlond, for his patience and understanding throughout this undertaking. For their helpful feedback and willingness to read and critique my manuscript, I thank preservationist Marc Cooper, formerly of the Historic District Landmarks Commission in New Orleans and now beginning his tenure as Director of the Vieux Carré Commission, and historian Dr. Randolph Delehanty, a once and (I hope) future collaborator who serves as curator of the Roger Houston Ogden Collection of Southern Art.

I especially thank my wife Rives, and daughters Adrianne and Claire, not only for putting up with me throughout this project during the trips back and forth to Sea Ranch and Seaside, but for being receptive and enthusiastic about every exploratory side trip down the road of life precipitated by my desire to learn more about architecture and community. These experiences ultimately culminated in this book.

Alexander, Christopher, Sara Ishikawa, and Murray Silverstein. *A Pattern Language*. New York: Oxford University Press, 1977.

Calthorpe, Peter. *The Next American Metropolis*. New York: Princeton Architectural Press, 1993.

Fishman, Robert. *Bourgeois Utopias: The Rise and Fall of Suburbia*. New York: Basic Books, 1987.

Fitzgerald, Frances. *Cities on a Hill*. New York: Simon and Schuster, 1981.

Garreau, Joel. *Edge City: Life on the New Frontier*. New York: Doubleday, 1991.

Jacobs, Jane. *The Death and Life of Great American Cities*. New York: Random House, 1961.

Keeler, Charles. *The Simple Home*. San Francisco: P. Elder, 1904. Reprint. Salt Lake City: Peregrine Smith, 1979.

Krieger, Alex, ed. *Andres Duany and Elizabeth Plater-Zyberk. Towns and Town Making Principles*. Cambridge: Harvard University Graduate School of Design, 1991.

Kunstler, James Howard. *The Geography of Nowhere*. New York: Simon & Schuster, 1993.

McAlester, Virginia and Lee. *A Field Guide to American Houses*. New York: Alfred A. Knopf, 1984.

Mohney, David, and Keller Easterling, eds. *Seaside: Making a Town in America*. New York: Princeton Architectural Press, 1991.

Moore, Charles; Donlyn Lyndon, and Gerald Allen. *The Place of Houses*. New York: Holt, Rinehart and Winston, 1974.

Mumford, Lewis. *The Culture of Cities*. New York: Harcourt, Brace, Jovanovich, 1938.

Neall, Lynne Creighton, ed. *Lawrence Halprin: Changing Places*. San Francisco: San Francisco Museum of Modern Art, 1986.

Oldenburg, Ray. *The Great Good Place*. New York: Paragon House, 1989.

Owens, Bill. *Suburbia*. San Francisco: Straight Arrow Books, 1972.

Papadakis, Andreas, ed. *Leon Krier: Houses, Palaces, Cities*. London: Architectural Design Editions Ltd., 1984.

Rybczynski, Witold. *Home: A Short History of an Idea*. New York: Viking/Penguin, 1986.

Scully, Vincent. *American Architecture and Urbanism*. Rev. ed. New York: Henry Holt, 1988.

Stern, Robert A. M., ed. *The Anglo-American Suburb*. London: Architectural Design, 1981.

Venturi, Robert; Denise Scott Brown and Steven Izenour. Rev. ed. *Learning From Las Vegas*. Cambridge: MIT Press, 1977.

Wolfe, Tom. *From Bauhaus to Our House*. New York: Farrar Straus Giroux, 1981.

Woodbridge, Sally, ed. *Bay Area Houses*. Salt Lake City: Peregrine Smith, 1988.

# SEA RANCH

POP. 280 · ELEV. 40

# SEASIDE
# TOWN LIMIT
# POP. 862
(CATS & DOGS INC.)

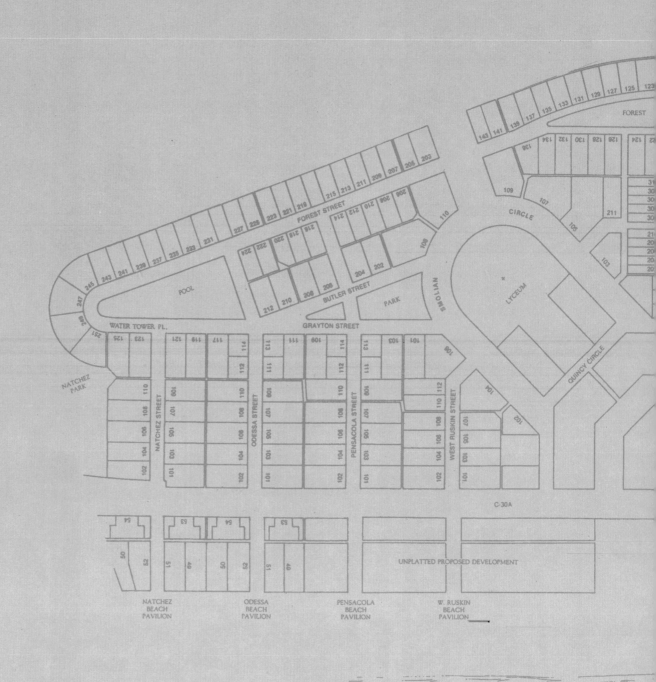